1800 CENSUS OF CALVERT COUNTY AND CHARLES COUNTY, MARYLAND

Maryland Genealogical Society, Inc.
T. Harvey Jones, Jr., President

HERITAGE BOOKS
2007

HERITAGE BOOKS
AN IMPRINT OF HERITAGE BOOKS, INC.

Books, CDs, and more—Worldwide

For our listing of thousands of titles see our website
at
www.HeritageBooks.com

Published 2007 by
HERITAGE BOOKS, INC.
Publishing Division
65 East Main Street
Westminster, Maryland 21157-5026

International Standard Book Number: 978-0-7884-3290-3

CHARLES COUNTY, MARYLAND

1800 CENSUS

By

MARYLAND GENEALOGICAL SOCIETY, INC.

Herman J. Heiger, President

3504 Essex Road, Baltimore, Maryland 21207

Copyright 1967

INTRODUCTION

Established in 1658, Charles County adjoins Saint Mary's County in the large peninsula between the Chesapeake Bay and the Potomac River. A portion of it was set off into the new Prince George's County in 1695. It is but a few miles across the Potomac River from the Virginia Northern Neck counties of Westmoreland, King George, Stafford, Prince William, and Fairfax.

In spite of the loss of certain records by fires in 1746 and 1892, most of the records are still preserved. For an inventory of county records, see Radoff et al, The County Courthouses and Records of Maryland, Part Two: The Records (Annapolis, 1963), pages 97-102. Though compulsory registration of vital records did not begin until 1865, the court clerk recorded births, marriages, and some deaths for the period 1654-1706 in the back of the first series of deed books, volumes C, P, and Q. A transcript of these early vital records was published by Robert F. Hayes, Jr., in Maryland Historical and Genealogical Bulletin, volumes 1 through 6 (Baltimore, 1930-1935). Charles County marriage licenses, 1777-1801, were published in G. M. Brumbaugh, Maryland Records, volume 2.

Abstracts of wills for the period 1665-1684 were published by Raymond B. Clark, Jr., in The Maryland and Delaware Genealogist, volume 6 and 7 (Washington 1965-1966). Court proceedings for the period 1658-1674 have been published in the Archives of Maryland, volumes 53 and 60. Newman's Charles County Gentry (1940) provided much information about the history and families of the county. General historical information is provided by Klapthor and Brown in History of Charles County (La Plata, 1958). Early rent rolls are among the Calvert Papers at the Maryland Historical Society, Baltimore, which also has transcripts of the Durham and the Trinity parish registers. Debt books are to be found at the Maryland Land Office at Annapolis. No records are extant for the Pickyawaxon Friends Meeting, which was organized by 1686. The register of the Patuxent Orthodox Friends Monthly Meeting is available from 1809 on microfilm at the Maryland Hall of Records, Annapolis.

In the 1790 Census of Maryland, there were 2,043 heads of families listed, with a total nonslave population of 10,528 persons. Names were arranged alphabetically, rather than by location in a specific hundred or parish. The following transcript of the 1800 Census is therefore the earliest census by parish. Because only five parishes are involved, viz., Durham, Port Tobacco, St. George's, Trinity, and William and Mary, we have not included an index, but have rearranged the names within each parish census in alphabetical order to facilitate reference use.

The following members of the Maryland Genealogical Society assisted in the transcribing, compiling, and preparation of this transcript:

Mrs. Gladys Keen; J. Harrison Daniels; and George Ely Russell.

This is the second in a series of Maryland 1800 Census publications by the Maryland Genealogical Society. The Calvert County, Maryland, 1800 Census was published in 1965. The third volume, Prince George's County, is now being prepared for publication.

George Ely Russell, C.G.

Head of the family	Free white males					Free white females					Other free persons	Number of slaves
	Under 10	10 - 16	16 - 26	26 - 45	Over 45	Under 10	10 - 16	16 - 26	26 - 45	Over 45		
ADDINGTON, Richard (a)	1			1					1		1	
ADDISON, James (c)	1			1		1			1	1	4	
ADDISON, Isabella (c)										1		
AMBLE, John (a)				1				1	1			
ALLEN, William (a)		1			1		1	1		1	6	
ALLNUTT, Edmond (c)	1			1		2	1	1			9	
ALLNUTT, James (c)					1			1		1	19	
ALLNUTT, Thomas (c)			1	1							2	
ALLNUTT, Zachariah (c)			1	1			1	3		1	7	
ALTON, Hezikiah (c)	1		1	1							2	
ANDERSON, Elizabeth (c)			1			1	2	2	1		10	8
ASKEW, John (c)	1			1		2	3	1	1			
ASKEW, Michael (c)		1	1	2		2	1	1		1		
ASKEW, William (c)				1						1		
ASKREW, William (a)		1			1	1		3				
AVIS, Ann (c)			1		1		1	1	1			1
AVIS, David (c)		2			1		2	1	1		5	
AVIS, John (c)		2		1								
BAKER, Betsey (c)						2	1		1			
BAKER, Isaac (no record) (c)												
BAKER, John (c)	2		1			2	1		1			
BAKER, Manning (a)			1			2	1	1				
BAKER, Thomas (c)			1			1	1					
BALLARD, Elizabeth (a)	1		1	1			1	1		1	10	1
BANETT, Daniel (c)	2				1		1	1	1			
BAREFORD, William (c)	2	1		1			2		1			
BARKER, George (a)				1					1		5	
BARKER, Stephen (a)				1		3		1	1			
BARNES, Mary (c)							1		1		5	
BEADEN, Jeremiah (c)				1		1		1			7	
BEADEN, Thomas (a)		1		1		1		1	1		6	
BECKET, John (a)		1		1		2	1		2		23	
BINNION (?) Thomas (c)	1		2	1	1	1	2	1		1	1	
BIRKHEAD, Nehemiah (a)	2	1	1	1		2	2			1		
BIRKHEAD, Sarah (c)									2	1		
BLACKBURN, Benjamin (c)			1			1	1	1	(torn)			
BLACKBURN, Benjamin (c)	1			1		1	2		1			
BLACKBURN, Charles (c)	1				1	1	2	1	1			
BLACKBURN, James (c)	1	1		1		4	1		1		2	
BLAIR, Lewis (a)			1		1	4			1		19	
BLAKE, Joseph (a)	1			1		4			1		28	3
BLAKE, Thomas (a)				1					1	1	5	
BOND, John (c)			1			2			1		27	
BOURNE, George (c)	1	1		1		2			1		9	
BOURNE, Sarah (c)										1	17	
BOURNE, Sarah, Jr. (c)			1			3		1			6	
BOURNE, Thomas (c)			1									2

Head of the family		Free white males					Free white females					Other free persons	Number of slaves
		Under 10	10 - 16	16 - 26	26 - 45	Over 45	Under 10	10 - 16	16 - 26	26 - 45	Over 45		
BOURNE, William	(c)	1	1	2						1		14	
BOURNS, Benjamin	(c)	3		1			(torn)						
BOWEN, Alexander	(c)	1		1			1		1				
BOWEN, Basil	(c)	1			1								
BOWEN, Benjamin G.	(c)				2		1		1				
BOWEN, Charles	(c)	3	2			1				1		8	
BOWEN, Isaac (of Isaac)	(c)	2	2	2	1		4	1			1		
BOWEN, Jacob	(c)					1		1			1		
BOWEN, Jane	(c)		1	1			1				1		
BOWEN, John	(c)		1	1	1		2			1			
BOWEN, Jonathan	(c)				1	1							
BOWEN, Margaret	(c)		2	1			1	1	1	1			
BOWEN, Mary	(c)			1	1				1	1	1	9	
BOWEN, Minty	(c)	1	2	3			2	1	2	1			
BOWEN, Parker	(c)		1	1		1			1		1	4	
BOWEN, Patrick	(c)		1	1					1	1		3	
BOWEN, Rebecca	(c)	1		1					1		1		
BOWEN, Samuel	(c)	2		3	1		1	1	1		1		
BOWEN, Walter	(a)	2	1		1		3			1		1	
BOWEN, William	(c)				1	1	1	1		1			
BOWEN, Young	(c)	1			1	1	1			1		4	
BOYED, John	(a)	1			1		1		1				
BRADY, John	(c)	1		1			1			1			
BREADING, Ann	(c)	1								1		1	
BREESE, Joanna	(a)	1	1				1	1		1			
BRINKLEY, William	(c)	2	2	2	1		1	2		1			
BRITTON, Elizabeth	(a)						2			1			
BROOKE, Basil	(c)		1			1		1	1	1		60	5
BROOME, Alisander	(c)	1				1				1		4	
BROOME, John	(c)			2	1				2			11	9
BROOME, Mary	(c)									1		23	
BROOMS, William D.	(c)	1	1		2		1	1		1	1	19	1
BROWN, James	(a)	3	2		1		2		1	1			
BROWN, Robert	(a)				1		1			1			
BUCKINGHAM, John	(c)		1			1			1	4	1		
BUCKMASTER, Henry	(c)	3	2		1				1	1			
CAR, Benja.	(a)				1		1						
CASEY, Betsey	(c)						1	1		1			
CAUCAND, Davide	(a)					1					1	17	
CAURCAND, William	(a)	1			1		1		2			13	5
CHAMBERS, Henry	(a)				1					1		1	13
CHAMBERS, Jacob	(c)	3	1		1					1		1	
CHAMBERS, James K.	(c)			1						1			
CHAMBERS, William	(a)	1			1		2			1			
CHANEY, Lewis	(a)			2						1		1	

Head of the family	Free white males					Free white females					Other free persons	Number of slaves
	Under 10	10 - 16	16 - 26	26 - 45	Over 45	Under 10	10 - 16	16 - 26	26 - 45	Over 45		
CHANEY, Sarah (a)			1			2			1		4	
CHANEY, Thomas (a)			1	1					1		5	
CHANEY, William, Jr.(a)	1	1	1			1			1			
CHANEY, William (a)	3	2	1			3			1			
CHARLTON, Edward (c)	1		1			1		2				
CHARLTON, James (c)			1				1		1			
CHARLTON, James, Jr.(c)		1	1			2			1			
CHARLTON, Thomas (c)	1		1				2		1			
CHEW, John (a)			1	1		1				1	29	1
CHEW, William (a)			1	1				1		1	17	
CHISLEY, John (c)	3	1	1	1		3	3		1		30	
CHISLEY, Thomas (c)	1			1		2			1		15	3
CHITTON, Richard (a)			1					2	1			
CLARE, Elizabeth (c)		2					2		1		1	
CLARE, John (c)		2			1	1	2	2	1	1	24	
CLARE, William (c)			1			1	1	1	1		5	5
COBRET, Rachel (c)			1	1					1			
COLE, Henry (c)	2			1		1				1		
CONNICK, Charles (c)			1					1	1	1		
CONWELL, John (a)	2	1		1		1	1		1			
CONWELL, Margaret (c)		1					2		1			
CONWELL, Susannah (a)	1					1			1			
COSTER, Benjamin (c)	2		1			1		1	1			1
COSTER, John (c)	1	1		1		2			1			
COTTINGTON, Elizabeth(a)		2						1		1		
COTTINGTON, Elizabeth(a)		1	1					1	1			
COTTINGTON, Jeremiah(a)	3			1					1			
COX, James (a)	1		2	1		2			1			
COX, Jeremiah (a)					1					2	4	
COX, Jeremiah (a)		1	1		1		1			1	6	
COX, Jeremiah 3 (a)	1	1		1		1	1	1				
COX, Theodore (c)	2	2	1	1			1		1		1	
COX, William (a)	1			1				1				
CRAIN, William (c)	1		1			1		1				
CRAIN, Thomas (c)	1	2	2		1	3	1	1	1			
CRANDFORD, James (a)	3			1		1	1		1		8	
CRANFORD, Clement (a)	1	2	1	1			1		1			
CROSBEY, Elizabeth (a)	1	2	2							1	2	
CROSBEY, Walter (a)	1			1				1			4	3
CROSBY, Richard (a)	3			1			1		1		1	
CULLEMBER, Jeremiah (c)					1		1		1			
CULLEMBER, Jesse (c)	3	2			1	3	2		1			
CULLEMBER, Nathaniel(c)	2	2			1			2		1		
CULLEMBER, Rebecca (c)		1				4	1		1			
CULLEMBER, Sarah (c)							1	1		1		
CULPPER, John (c)		1									10	1
CURR, John (a)	1				1	1	2		1			

4

Head of the family	Free white males					Free white females					Other free persons	Number of slaves
	Under 10	10 - 16	16 - 26	26 - 45	Over 45	Under 10	10 - 16	16 - 26	26 - 45	Over 45		
DARE, Gideon (c)	2	3	2		1		2	2	1	1		28
DARE, John (a)	1		1		1	1	1		1		20	1
DARE, Thomas (a)	1		1			2			1		5	
DARE, Nathaniel (c)			1		1			4	1	1	30	
DARYMPLS, John (a)	3			1		1			1			
DARYMPLS, William (c)	2			1		1	3		1		17	
DAWKINS, Alesander (c)	1	3		1	1	1	3		1		39	
DAWKINS, Charles (c)	1	1			1	1		1	1		12	
DAVID, Joseph (a)	1			1		3	2	1	1		2	
DAVIS, Benjamin (a)	2			1		2			1			
DAY, Benja. (c)	1	1			1	1		1	1		12	
DAY, Robert (c)	3			1		1	1		1	1	15	
DAY, William (c)		1		1							1	
DEAL, John (a)	2		1	1				2				
DEAL, William (a)			2		1			2			1	
DEAL, WILLIAM Jr. (a)	1			1			1		1		7	
DEAVOR, James (c)			1			2			1		1	
DENTON, John (c)			2	1	1	2		2	1			
DENTON, Thomas (c)	3	2		1	1	1			1			
DESHEALDS, Benjamin (a)	1	1	1		1	1		1				
DEVON, Thomas (a)	1			1		2			1			
DIMONT, Michael (c)	2	2			1	2			1			
DIXON, Benjamin (c)				3	2				1		5	
DIXON, Catey (c)	2	2				2			1			
DIXON, Joseph (c)			1					1				
DIXON, William (c)		1		(torn)								
DORSEY, Benjamin (c)			1			1		1				
DORSEY, Daniel (a)	1			1		1		1				
DORSEY, Francis (a)	2	1		1		2	1		1			
DORSEY, James (c)	1	1	1	2			1	1		1	2	
DORSEY, James (of James) (a)	4	2			1	1	1		1		2	
DORSEY, James (of John) (a)				2			1	1		2		
DORSEY, James (of Joseph) (c)	1			1		1		1	1			
DORSEY, Joseph (c)		3	1		1							
DORSEY, Philip (a)					1						10	
DORSEY, Philip Jr. (c)	2	1		1		3	2		1			
DORSEY, Samuel (c)	2	1		1			2		1		20	
DORSEY, Somerset (c)				1		4	1		1			
DORSEY, Thomas (c)	2			2		1			1		7	
DORSEY, Young (a)	1			1		2			1		2	
DOTSON, Benjamin (c)	2	1		1		3			1			
DOTSON, Ellenor (c)	1					1		1	1	1	(worn)	
DOWELL, Harrison (c)	3	1		1		2		1				
DOWELL, Henry (a)	2			1		2			1		3	

Head of the family	Free white males					Free white females					Other free persons	Number of slaves
	Under 10	10 - 16	16 - 26	26 - 45	Over 45	Under 10	10 - 16	16 - 26	26 - 45	Over 45		
DOWELL, John (a)	3	2	2		1	1			1	1	3	
DOWELL, John (a)	2	2			1		1	2	2		1	
DOWELL, Mary (a)			1	2			1		1		7	
DOWELL, Susannah (a)			1					1		1		
DUKE, Mary (c)				1				1		1	10	
EADES, Sinnea (a)						2	1		1			
EADES, Thomas (a)	2		1		1			2	1			
EARLE, John (a)			1			1		1	1		1	
EDES, Isaac (a)			1		1	2			1			
ELLISON, Charles (a)				1					1	1	8	
EMMERSON, Peter (a)	1		1	1					1		..	
EMONDS, Dolley (a)	1	1		2			1	1	1		2	
EOCUT (?) Benjamin (a)	2	1		1		1			1			1
ESSIS, Elizabeth (a)	2	2		1		2		2	2	1	3	
ESSIS, John (a)				1		2	1		1			
ESSIS, Joseph Jr. (a)	1	1	1	1		2	2	2	1			
ESSIS, Joseph (a)	2	2		1		2		1				
ESSIS, Isaac (a)				1		2		1				2
ESSIS, SAMUEL (a)	3			1		2		1	1			
ESSIS, William (a)	2	1		1		1		1				
ESLIP, Heason (a)		1	2	1		2		1	1		19	
EVERETTE, Abbey (a)				1				1			19	
EVINS, Joseph (a)	1		1			1		2				
EVINS, Thomas (a)	2	2	1			2		1	1			
EVINS, William (a)			2	1							17	2
FIBBENS, Joseph (a)				1			1		1			
FITZHUGH, John (a)	3			1	1	1		2	1		48	
FOWLER, Jessie (c)		1	2		1		1	1	1			
FOWLER, Joseph (c)	2	1		1				1		1		
FOWLER, William (c)	(page worn on bottom)	1		1								
FRAIZER, Daniel (a)	1			1				1	1		4	
FRAZER, James H. (c)	2			1		2			1		8	
FRAIZER, Pamelia (a)	2					3		1	1		22	1
FREELAND, Benj. (a)	3			1		1			1		6	
FREELAND, Francis (a)						1		1			13	
FREELAND, Frisby (a)	1	1			1		1	2		1	56	
FREELAND, Frisby, Jr. (a)	1		1						1		15	
FREELAND, Joseph (a) (of Robert)	2			1				1			11	
FREELAND, Peregin (a)			2		1			2			22	4
FREELAND, Robert (a)		1	1	2							16	
FREELAND, Thomas (a)				1							12	
FREEMAN (worn) (a)	(worn)				2	5			1		1	
FREEMAN, Chaney (a)		1					1	2		1	12	
FREEMAN, Mary (a)	2					1	1		2		8	

Head of the family	Free white males					Free white females					Other free persons	Number of slaves
	Under 10	10 - 16	16 - 26	26 - 45	Over 45	Under 10	10 - 16	16 - 26	26 - 45	Over 45		
FREEMAN, Thomas (a)	1	1	1		1	1	2					
FRENCH, Benj. (a)	1			1		2			1			
FRENCH, Jacob (a)				1				1				1
FRY, Elizabeth (a)						1			1	1	3	
FRY, Gantilen (a)				1		2			1			
FRYER, William (c)	2			1			1	1			1	
GALLOWAY, John (a)	1			1		3			1			
GALLOWAY, Sarah (a)	2	1					3		1			
GAMES, Isaac (c)				1		1	1	1	1			
GAMES, Sarah (c)	4				1	3	3		2		11	
GAMTT (JANTT) Edward (c)		1		1							53	
GANTT, Thomas Jr. (a)	1	2			1				1		29	
GARDNER, Benj. (c)			1					1				
GARDNER, Benj. P. (c)			1					1				
GARDNER, John (c)	2			1				2	1			
GARDNER, Rebecca (c)		1	1					1	1	1		
GIBSON, JAMES (a)	3	2		1		1		1			8	
GIBSON, John (a)	3	1		1		1	2		1			
GIBSON, Peter (a)	3			1		1			1	1	1	
GIBSON, Richard (a)				1		1		1	1		1	
GIBSON, Samuel (a)	1			1				1	1			
GIBSON, Samuel Jr. (a)	2			1		1	1	1			4	2
GOTT, Ann (c)	1		2				1	1	1		5	
GOVER, Robert (a)		1		1				1	2		7	
GRAHAM, Asenath (a)			1	1					1	1	53	
GRAY, Alisand (c)		1		1		1			1			
GRAY, Elizabeth (a)	1	1	1				2		1		12	
GRAY, Elizabeth (c)	1	1					1			1	13	
GRAY, George (c)			1						1	1	4	
GRAY, Henrey (?) (c)					1	1			1		3	2
GRAY, Dr. James (c)	1	3			1	2			1		32	1
GRAY, Thomas (BG) (c)				1	1				1		16	
GRAY, Thomas (c)	3			1		1			1		9	
GRAY, Thomas Esq. (c)		1			1	1	1	1		1	43	1
GREEVER, Hezekah (c)			1	1		1	1	1				
GRIFFIN, Benj. (a)			2	1		1	1	1				
GRIFFIN, Rebecca (c)						1	1	1	2		1	
GRIFFESS, Joseph (c)				1					1		13	1
GRIFFISS, John (c)				1					1			
GROSIDFIELD, Walter (c)				1		1			1		9	
GROVER, Thomas (c)	1	2		1		1	1		1			
GROVER, Robert (c)				1					1			
HALL, Henry (a)	2			1		1			1			
HALL, John (a)	1			1					1	(worn)		
HALL, Joseph (c)	2				1			1		1		

Head of the family	Free white males					Free white females					Other free persons	Number of slaves
	Under 10	10 - 16	16 - 26	26 - 45	Over 45	Under 10	10 - 16	16 - 26	26 - 45	Over 45		
HALL, William (c)			1		1	3		1		1		
HALL, Zacheriah (c)	1	1		1		2			1			
HALL, Zacheriah (c)	2			1					1			
HALL, -- John (c)	1		1				1	1				
HANCE, Elisha (c)	1			1		1			2	1	7	
HANCE, Francis (c)	1	1		1		2	1		1		17	
HANCE, Joseph (c)	1			1		1	3		1		4	
HANCE, Kinsey (c)				1					1	1	14	1
HANCE, Richard (c)	2			1		3	1		1		5	
HANES, Benjamin (c)			1				2	2		2	21	
HANES, Benjamin (c) (of John)	1				1	2	1	1	1		18	
HANES, Benjamin (c)	1		2	1			2		1			10
HANES, Joseph (c)	1			1				1	1	1	2	
HANES, Richard (a)	1			1		2	1	1	1		3	
HANES, Thomas (a)	1			1		1			1			
HANISON, Sarah (a)		2	1			2		1		1		
HARDACRE, James (a)	2	2		1				1		2	6	
HARDESTY, Ann (a)						1				2		3
HARDESTY, Daniel (a)			1	1		2		1		1		
HARDESTY, James (a)					1					1		
HARDESTY, Richard (a)	1			1		1		1				
HARDESTY, Thomas (a)		1		1		2			1			
HARDESTY, William (a)	1			1		1	1		1			
HARDESTY, William,Jn.(a)			1	1			2					
HARDISTY, Jesse (a)				1		3			1		1	
HARDISTY, Joseph (c)	2	1			1		1		1		6	
HARDISTY, Joseph, Jr. (a)			2	1				1		1	3	
HARDISTY, Rebecca (a)						1		1				
HARRIS, Jacob (a)	3		1	1		2	3			1	1	
HARRIS, Joseph (c)		2	1	1				1			13	
HARRIS, Joseph, Jr. (a)			2	1				1		1	3	
HARRIS, William (c)	3	1			1	2			1		12	
HARRISON, Charles (a)	1		1			1	2		1		3	1
HARRISON, Henry (a)	3				1				1	1		
HARRISON, James (a)			1	1						1		
HARRISON, James, Jr.(a)			1					1				
HARRISON, Lewis (c) (HARISSON?)		1		1		1		1				
HARRISON, Richard (a)	2		1	1		2			1		3	11
HARRISON, Robert (a)	2	2	1		1		1	4	1	1	3	
HARRISON, Samuel (a)		1			1		1	1			1	
HARRISON, Thomas (a)	1			1		4			1		3	
HARRISON, William (a)		1		1				2	1		3	
HARRISON, William (a)		1		1				2	1		3	
HARRISON, William,Jn(a)	1			1		3			1			
HARWOOD, Richard (c)				1							9	

Head of the family		Free white males					Free white females					Other free persons	Number of slaves
		Under 10	10 - 16	16 - 26	26 - 45	Over 45	Under 10	10 - 16	16 - 26	26 - 45	Over 45		
HARWOOD, Thomas	(a)	1	1	1		1			1	1		11	
HEIGHT ----	(a)	1		1			1		1			16	
HEIGHT, James	(c)			1	1			1	1	1		44	
HELLEN, Elizabeth	(c)	1		1					1		1	4	1
HELLEN, Jacob	(c)			2		1			3		1		
HELLEN, Jonathan	(c)				1	1							
HELLEN, Mary (of Walter)	(c)				1	1			1	1	1	14	?
HELLEN, Searth	(c)					1					1	8	
HELLEN, Thomas	(c)	3			1				1			6	1
HILLEN, James (or HELLEN)	(c)	1				1	1	1	3	1		3	
HILLEN, John I.	(c)			2	1							4	
HINTON, Josias	(c)	2	1	1	1				1	1		1	
HINTON, Mary	(a)	2		1			1	1		1			
HINTON, Richard	(a)		1		1		2				1		
HODGEKINS, Theodore	(a)	3	1		1		2	1	1			8	
HOLDEN, Ann	(a)			1			1		2		1		
HOLLAND, William	(a)	2			1		2			1		22	1
HOLLINGHEAD, Eliz.	(c)	1			2					1	1	11	
HOLLINGSHEAD, John	(a)		1		1		2		1	1		5	
HOLLINGSHEAD, John	(c)	2			1		1			1			
HOLT, Francis	(a)				2							11	7
HOLT, Philip	(a)	3	1			1				1		8	
HOMES, Anthony	(a)	1			1		1			1			
HOOPER, Isaac	(c)	3	1	3		1	1		1	1		5	1
HOOPER, Jacob	(c)	2		1	1		2			1		6	1
HOOPER, Mary	(a)		1						1		1		
HOOPER, Thomas	(c)	1		1					1				
HOPKINS, Ellenor	(a)		1				1	1		1		3	
HOWARD, John	(a)			1		1	1			1			
HOWARD, John, Jr.	(a)	1		1			1			1			
HOWARD, Richard	(a)	1				1	2			1			
HOWARD, William	(a)			1	1		3	1		1			
HOWARD, Thomas	(a)	1			1		3	1		1			
HOWS, Ann	(a)	2					1				1		
HOWS, Elisha	(a)	2			2		3	1		1		1	
HUNGERFORD, James	(c)	1	2		1	(worn)		1		(worn)			
HUNTT, Elizabeth	(a)								1		1		
HUNTT, Henry	(a)			2		1			2		1	13	
HUNTT, John W.	(a)		1	1		1		1	2		1	1	
HUNTT, Mary	(c)	1	1				2			2			
HUNTT, Orton	(c)			1					1				
HUNTT, Thomas	(a)	2			1		2		1		1		
HUTCHINS, Ann	(c)	3	2	1			1	2		1			
HUTCHENS, Catey	(c)						2		1		1		
HUTCHINS, John	(c)					1	2			1		5	1

Head of the family	Free white males					Free white females					Other free persons	Number of slaves
	Under 10	10 - 16	16 - 26	26 - 45	Over 45	Under 10	10 - 16	16 - 26	26 - 45	Over 45		
HUTCHENS, Sarah (c)		1	2				1		1	1	8	
HUTCHENS, Thomas (c)		1	1		1				2			
HUTCHENS, Thomas (c)			1			1	1					
IRELAND, John, Jr. (c)				1					1		30	
IRELAND, Richard (c)					1			2			19	
JACLAND (?), Gideon (c)		1		1							8	
JEFFERSON, Basil (c)	1			1		2			1		7	
JENKINS, Thomas (c)	1			1			1	1			14	
JOCCY, John (c)				1				1			2	
JOHNS, Benjamin (c) (of A.)	1	1			1	1	1	1	1		19	
JONES, Benjamin (a)	2	1	1	2		1	1	2	1		11	
JONES, Davide	2		1					1		1		1
JONES, James (a)				1		5	2	1		1	3	1
JONES, Thomas (a)	1		2		1	1		2		1	6	1
IRELAND, GILBERT (a)		1						1		1		1
IRELAND, John (c)				2	1				1	1	18	
IRELAND, Mary (c)	2			2				1	1		9	8
IRELAND, William (a)	2			1				1	1		3	
IRELAND, Richard Jr. (a)	2		2	1		1			1		15	
ISAACHE, Richard (a)	1	1			1			2	1			12
KENDEL, Margaret (c)						2		1	1	1	6	
KENTT, Daniel (c)		2		1	1	4		1	2	1	37	2
KENTT, Gideon (c)				1	1			2			1	
KENTT, Richard (c)	3	1		2		2			1		12	
KERSHAW, Francis (c)	3		1	1		1	1		1		2	
KERSHAW, James (c)		1		1		3		1	1			
KING, Benjamin (c)	2	1			2					1	52	
KING, Elizabeth (c)	1							1				
KING, Henry (c)				1		2		1				
KING, John (c)		1		1			2	1		1		
KING, Richard (c)				1		2	1	1				
KING, Thomas (c)				1		3		1		1	2	
LACEY, Stephen (a)		1		1		2	1		1		4	1
LAMB, John (a)					1					1		
LAMBERT, William (a)		1	1		1			1		1	1	
LANDSLEY, John (a)		1			1		1			1	1	
LANE, Hester (Miss) (a)						1				1	1	
LAURENS, John (a)	3	1		1			1		1		6	
LAURENS, Wm. (a)			1	1					2		10	
LE---LLE, John (c)				1				1	1		3	
LEACH, Asea (a)					1					1	2	

Head of the family		Free white males					Free white females					Other free persons	Number of slaves
		Under 10	10 - 16	16 - 26	26 - 45	Over 45	Under 10	10 - 16	16 - 26	26 - 45	Over 45		
LEACH, Benjamin	(c)	2			1		2	1		1			
LEACH, Benjamin	(a)			1			1		1				
LEACH, Joshua	(a)	3	2		1					1	1		
LECOIS, William	(c)		1		1					1		5	1
LEE, Robert	(a)		1			1			1		1	78	
LEUCILLE, John T.	(c)	2			1		1		1	1		6	
LEUCILLE, Rebecca	(c)			1							1		
LISBY, John	(c)		1	1		1			2		1		
LOGAN, John	(a)				1		2	2					
LOGLES, Ann	(a)		1								1		
LOU, Abriham	(c)		1	2		1	1			1		8	
LYLES, James	(a)	1			1		3			1			
LYLES, Samuel	(a)			1		1				1		6	2
LYLES, Thomas H.	(a)	2	1		1		2	1		1		17	
LYLES, William (of Thos.)	(a)	1			1		3						
LYLES, William	(a)		1		1	1	1	1	1		1		
McDOWELL, John	(c)				1						1	4	
McGUIRE, John	(a)	1			1		3	1		1		1	
McKAY, Elijah	(a)	1	3		1		1			1		2	1
McKINSEY, Cossemer	(c)	1			1		2			1		5	
McRAY, George	(a)					1			2				
MACKALL, Ge. Benj.	(c)					1					1	38	
MACKALL, Benj. H.	(c)	2			1		1		1			24	
MACKALL, Hanner	(c)										1	19	
MACKALL, James	(a)					1			2		1	5	
MACKALL, John (of B.)	(c)	1			1		4		1	1		9	
MACKALL, John G.	(c)			1	1							43	4
MACKALL, Levin	(c)				1		1	1		1		41	
MACKALL, Richard	(a)			1	1		1		1			24	1
MACKALL, Walter	(c)				1			1				30	2
MARGUIS (torn)						(worn)							
MARQUIS, William	(a)	3	1			1	3			1			
MEADS, Ann	(a)			2				1			1	5	
MEADS, Jackson	(a)			1			1		1			2	
MELLEY, Hillary	(c)			1			1	1		1		7	
MELLEY, Moses	(c)	2	1		1					1		7	
MERCHANT, Geo.	(c)	1	1		1					1			
MILLER, David	(c)	1				1			2	1			
MILLER, John	(a)		2			1		1	1				
MILLER, John Jr.	(c)					1		3	1	2			
MILLS, Ann	(c)	2	1	1			1				1	20	
MILLS, John	(c)			1	1							16	
MILLS, John (of Leon)	(c)	1		1					2	2		10	

Head of the family	Free white males					Free white females					Other free persons	Number of slaves
	Under 10	10 - 16	16 - 26	26 - 45	Over 45	Under 10	10 - 16	16 - 26	26 - 45	Over 45		
MILLS, Leonard (c)					1				1		9	
MITCHELL, John (a)	3			1				2				
MITCHELL, Willey (a)	1						1			1	3	
MOORE, Edward (c)				1					1			
MOORE, Thomas (c)	1			1		2	1		1		13	
MORGAN, Jonathan (c)	3	1			1	2	1		1			
MORGAN, Mary (c)	1					1	1		1	1	22	
MORSELL, James (a)				2	1	1				1		
MORSELL, John (c)	2			1		2			1			
MORSELL, Susannah (c)								1	1			
MULES, Eleanor (a)	1					2	2		1		6	
MULES, Samuel (a)				1		1		1			1	
MULES, Thomas (a)	3			1		3			1		(torn)	
MUNNETT, Ann (c)	2		1			1	2		1			
MUNNITT (?) Abriham (c)	1			1		1			1		5	
NORFOLK, John (a)	1	2		1				1				
NORFOLK, John (of Is.) (a)	2			1		1		1	1		5	
NORFOLK, Isaac (a)			2	1					1			
NORFOLK, Richard (a)	1			1		2			1			
NORFOLK, Samuel (a)				1		5	1		1			
NORFOLK, Thomas (a)	3			1		1			1			
NORFOLK, William (a)	2		1	1		1	1		1			
NORFOLK, William (of Isaac) (a)	2	2			1	2			1		1	13
NORWELL, Gilbert (a)			1		1			1		1	4	
NORWELL, John (a)			2		1	1	1	1		1		
NORWELL, Richard (a)					1		2	1				
NOWELL, William (a)		1			1	3	3		1			
OGDON, Aaron (a)	2			1		1		1			7	
OGDON, Charles (a)				1			1		1			
OGDON, Moses (a)	2			1		1			1			
OGDON, Priscilla (a)	2	1				2		1				
OGDON, William (a)				1			1	1				
(above sometimes spelled ODGON)												
OSTERN, Richard (a)	1			1		1		1			6	
OWENS, Betty (a)	1		1				1	1		1	6	
OWENS, Samuel (a)	1			2		1	1	1	1			
PANAN, Alexander (c)	3		2		1	3	2	1	1		11	
PANAN, Elizabeth (c)	1		1		1	1	1	2		1		
PANAN, Richard (c)	1		1					1			4	
PANAN, Thomas (a)	3	1	1	1		2	2	1	1		15	
PANTRY, John (a)		1	3					2				

Head of the family	Free white males					Free white females					Other free persons	Number of slaves
	Under 10	10 - 16	16 - 26	26 - 45	Over 45	Under 10	10 - 16	16 - 26	26 - 45	Over 45		
PARDOC, Margaret (c)		1	1					2		1	1	
PARKER, Alexander (a)				1		1			1		4	
PARKER, Fielder (a)	2		1	1		1			1			
PARKER, Fielder Jr. (a)				1							7	
PARKER, George (a)	2			1		3	1	3	1		3	
PARKER, George (of G.) (a)	1	1		1		1			1			
PARKER, Marsham (a)	4			1		1			1		11	2
PARKER, Mary (c)									1		30	
MARKER, Mar--- Jr. (a)				1			(torn)			1		
PARKER, Susannah (a)							1		1			
PARKER, William (c)			1						1			
PASTERS, Christian (c)					2		1			1		
PATTISON, Jeremiah (c)					1					1	8	
PATTISON, John (a)			1		1		3			1	9	1
PEPPLOC, John (c)			2			1		1				
PETERS, Issebella (a)			1			2			1		5	
PITCHER, John (c)	1		1			1		1				
PITCHER, Samuel (c)	1		1					1				
PITCHER, Young (c)			2					1		1		
PLATFORD, Francis (a)		1					1		1		4	2
PLATFORD, Martha (a)		1				1		1			1	
POOL, Edmond (a)	1			1		2			1			
POOL, John (a)	2			1		1			1	1		
POOL, Joseph (a)				1				1			17	
POOL, William (a)				1		2			1			
POPLE, Samuel (a)	4	1		1		1			1			1
POWELL, William (c)		1			1				1	1	6	
PRICE, Dorsea (c)		1							1	1	4	
PRICE, James (a)				1					1			
PRICE, John (c)				1		1			1			1
PRICE, William (c)	1		1		1	1	2		1			
PROUT, Richard (a)	2	1		1		2	1		1		3	
PYBUS, James					1						4	
RAMSEY, George (c)	1			1		1			1			
RAMSEY, William (c)		1		1		1	2		1			
RANDAL, Jeremiah (c)	1				1	1			1			
RAWLINGS, Aaron (a)	1			1		2		1			4	
RAWLINGS, Daniel (c)				1							4	
RAWLINGS, CaptJoseph (c)	1	1	1			1	1	3	1	1	38	
RAWLINGS, William (a)	2			1		1			1		18	
RENYOLDS, Edward (a)	1	2	2	1	1	2	1	1	1		58	12
REYNOLDS, Thomas (a)				1				1	1		18	
REYNOLDS, William (a)				1		3	1		1		28	5
RHODES, Abraham (c)			1		1	1		2			7	3
RHODES, Isaac (c)	2	1	1	1		1			1		5	

Head of the family	Free white males					Free white females					Other free persons	Number of slaves
	Under 10	10 - 16	16 - 26	26 - 45	Over 45	Under 10	10 - 16	16 - 26	26 - 45	Over 45		
RHODES, Thomas (a)	2		1	1						1	6	
RIGGINS, Basil (a)	1			1			3			1		
RIGHT, William (a)	1			1			1					
RIGHT, William Jr. (a)	1			1					1	1		
ROBERSON, Joseph (c)	2		1				1	1		1		
ROBERSON, John (c)	2			2		3	2		1	1	21	
ROBERTS, Ann (c)		1				1	1	1	1			
ROD, Hery (a)			1		1	1	1	1	1			
ROSS, Alesander (a)	3			1		2	1		1			
ROSS, Abriham (a)	4	1		1			1		1			
ROSS, Daniel (a)			1		1	1						
ROSS, Mary (a)			1	1		1	2			1	1	
SANDERLAND, Ann (a)	2							1	1		8	
SANDERLAND, Basil (a)			1						1		6	
SANDERLAND, Benjamin (a)	2					1			1		5	
SANDERLAND, Eliz. (a)	2					1			1		8	1
SANDERLAND, Josias (a)	4					1			1	1	7	
SANDERLAND, Reason B. (a)			1			1			1			
SEARS, William (a)		1		1		3				1	7	5
SEDWICKS, John (a)			1			2		1		1	10	
SEDWICKS, Joshua (a)		1		1						1	13	5
SEWELL, James (a)			2		1				3	1	7	
SEWELL, James, Jr. (a)	1			1		1					2	
SHEARS, Henry (a)	2	1	2	1	1	1	1		1		2	
SHEARS, Richard (a)	2		1	1		1			1		1	
SHRIOC, Richard (a)	2			1		2		1	1		1	
SHRIOC, Samuel (a)		1			1						1	
SHRIOC, Samuel, Jr. (a)	1			1		1		1			1	
SILWEN, Philip (a)	2	1		1		1	1			1	1	
SIMMONS, Basil (c)			1	1						1	31	
SIMMONS, Isaac (c)	2			1		3			1			1
SIMMONS, Mary (a)	2	1		1		1	1		1		(worn)	
SIMMONS, M--- (a)		1		1					1	1	16	
SIMMONS, Thomas (a)				1					1	1	1	1
SINCLAIR, William (a)	1		1	2			1			1	2	1
SKINNER, Clement (c)					1		1				2	
SKINNER, Frederick (c)	1	2	1					2	1	2	30	
SKINNER, James (c)								1	1		(worn)	
SKINNER, John (c)								1	3	2	17	
SKINNER, Richard		1	2			1		1	2	1	10	
SKINNER, Sarah (a)	1					1			1	1		1
SLATES, Daniel (a)	2					1			1	1		
SMITH, Dolly (a)	1	1				1		2	1		18	
SMITH, Fielder B. (a)			1	1		1			1		11	
SMITH, Gavin H. (a)		1	1	1	1	1		1	1			1
SMITH, George (a)	2				1	3			1			

Head of the family	Free white males					Free white females					Other free persons	Number of slaves
	Under 10	10 - 16	16 - 26	26 - 45	Over 45	Under 10	10 - 16	16 - 26	26 - 45	Over 45		
SMITH, John (a)	1	1		1		1		1				
SMITH, John H. (a)			1	1		2		1				
SMITH, Mordica (a)	3	1		1					1		9	
SMITH, Mordica F. (a)		1	3				1		1	1	11	1
SMITH, Nathaniel (a)			2		1			2	1		9	
SMITH, Susannah (a)				1				1	2		22	
SMITH, Walter (a)	1	1	1					2	4		10	
SMITH, William (a)			1			1		2			59	1
SMITH, William (a)			2						3			
SMOTHERS, Grig (c)					1				2			
SMOTHERS, James (a)	1			1					2			
SOLLARS, James M. (a)		1	1		1	2			2		30	
SOMERVILL, John (a)			1	1					1		11	
SOMERVILL, Rebecca (a)									1	1	36	
SOMERVILL, William (a)			1	1		1				1	16	
SPENCER, Francis (a)	1		1			1		2		1	7	
SPENCER, William (a)	1		1			2		1		1	1	4
SPICKNALL, John (a)	3	1			1	2			1		10	
SPICKNALL, John, Jr. (a)	4	1		1		2			1		3	
STALLINGS, Henry (a)	3			1		1			1		2	
STALLINGS, James (a)	1		1									
STALLINGS, John (a)	4	1		1		1			1			
STALLINGS, William (a)	1		1	1		1		1	1			
STALLINGS, William (a)	1	1		1		1	3		1			
STAMP, Francis (a)						1			1	1	4	
STAMP, Stephen (a)	1		1	1		1		1	1	1	3	
STANFORD, John (a)	3	1				1				1		
STANFORD, Joseph (a)	2	2			1	1			1			
STINNETT, William (a)	4	2		1		1		1	2			
STATTINGS, Peregin (a)	4			1			1		1		1	
STONE, James (a)				2	1	2	1			1	6	
STRICKNALL, Hardesty (a)	2			1		1		1				
STRICKNALL, Henry (a)				1		1	1		1			
STRICKNALL, Joseph (a)			1		1							
SURVERIEN, Dennis (a)	1			1		3			1		1	
SWAMPSTEAD, Nicholas (a)		4		1		2		1	1			
TALBERT, Elizabeth (c)		1	1						1		8	1
TALBERT, George (c)	2		1						1			
TALBERT, Philip (c)	2		1						1			
TALBERT, Thomas (c)	3				1			2		1	4	
TANEY, Michel (c)	1		2					3	1	1	(torn)	
TANNER, Mary (c)	2	2	1	1				1	2	1		
TAYLOR, Alisander (a)		1	2			2		1		1	16	
TAYLOR, Barbara (c)			2							1		
TAYNAHILL, Ann (a)	1	1								1		
TAYNAHILL, John (a)	3	1		1		1		3	1		6	4

Head of the family	Free white males					Free white females					Other free persons	Number of slaves
	Under 10	10 - 16	16 - 26	26 - 45	Over 45	Under 10	10 - 16	16 - 26	26 - 45	Over 45		
TAYNAHILL, Thomas (a)		1		1		2			2			
TAYNAHILL, William (a)	1			1		1				1		
TROTT, Nicholos (a)		1	1	2		2		1	1	1		
TROTT, Sabrel (a)	1	3	3		1		1			1		2
TUCKER, John (c) (of B)	1	1		1		1	1	1				
TUCKER, Rebecca (c)		1					1	1			(worn)	
TURNER, Ellenor (a)		1							1	1	2	
TURNER, John (c)				1				1	1		24	4
TURNER, Kid (c)	2			1		3			1		4	
TURNER, Richard (a)	3	2			1			1	1		3	
TURNER, Thomas (a)	2				1	4	1	4	1			
TURNER, William (a)	1	1		1		1		2	1			
TURNER, Wm. Jr. (a)	2			1				1	1	1		
TURNER, William (of Rich.) (a)	1			1		1				1		
TRAVIS, Elenor (c)		2						1	2	1	11	1
TRUMAN, Edward (c)	1			1		1						
WARD, Benjamin (a)				1							2	
WARD, James (c)	1			1					1			
WARD, Jack (?) (a)	1		1					1	1		4	
WARD, Robert (a)	1		1			2			1		4	
WARD, Sam'l. (a)			1						2		4	
WATSON, Benjamin (a)			1			1			1		2	
WATSON, David (a)	1	1	1		1	2	2		1	1		
WATSON, William (a)	1		2		1			1	1	1	10	
WEDGE, Belle (c)						1	1			1		
WEEMS, James Sr. (c)					1	1	1		2		31	
WEEMS, James Jr. (c)				1		1		1	1		2	
WEEMS, Wm. S. or L. (a)				1							16	3
WEEMS, Isaac (a)				1						2	10	4
WEEMS, Lock (a)				1					1		8	
WEEMS, William (a)			1	1								
WELLS, William (a)	2	2			1	3	1		1		6	1
WEST, Ruben (c)					1	1			1			
WHITTINGTON, Francis (a)		1	2		1			2		1	9	
WHITTINGTON, James (a)					1	1				1	10	
WHITTINGTON, James Jr. (a)	2		1	1					1			
WHITTINGTON, James Jr. (a)	2			1		3	2		1			
WHITTINGTON, Mary (a)			2	1			1		1			
WHITTINGTON, Samuel (a)			1	2		1			1		4	
WHITTINGTON, William (a)	4				1	1			1		7	
WILEY, John (a)				1		2	1		1		2	
WILKINSON, Elizabeth (c)				1		1			1	1	13	
WILKINSON, Henry (c)	2	1		1					1	1		
WILKINSON, John (c)		1	3		1	1	1	3			1	
WILKINSON, Joseph (a)	1	1	4	1	1		2	1		2	40	

Head of the family	Free white males					Free white females					Other free persons	Number of slaves
	Under 10	10 - 16	16 - 26	26 - 45	Over 45	Under 10	10 - 16	16 - 26	26 - 45	Over 45		
WILKINSON, Joseph (a) (of P.)	1	1		1		3		1	1			
WILKINSON, Philip (a)				1				1				
WILKINSON, Richard (c)		2		1					1	1	1	
WILKINSON, William		1		1				1				
WILKINSON, Young (c)		1			1	2	1	1			5	1
WILLIAMS, Benjamin (c)			1	1		1		1			15	
WILLIAMS, Francis (c)	2		1			1		1				
WILLIAMS, John (c)		(blotted)							1		(blotted)	
WILLIAMS, John H. (c)	3			1		2	1	1				
WILLIAMS, John P. (c)	1	2						1	1		5	
WILLIAMSON, Charles (a)	1	2	2		1	2		3	1	1	22	1
WILLS (WELLS) Joseph (a)	4	1		1				1				
WILSON, Andrew (c)					1			1			2	
WILSON, Benjamin (c)	3	1		1		1	1	1			1	9
WILSON, Elizabeth (c)	1							1		1		9
WILSON, James (a)			1	1				1				
WILSON, James (c) (of Jos.)	2			1				1			9	
WILSON, Joseph (c) (of Jos.)	2	1		1		1	1	1				
WILSON, Joseph (c) (of Th.)				1		2		1			14	
WILSON, Thomas (a)	1	1	2	1				1	1	1	29	
WINFIELD, Francis (a)	1	1				1			1	1	8	
WINNEL, John (c)	1			1		3	1	1				
WINSIT, John (c)	2	1	1	1		2		1	1			
WOLF, Francis (c)	1	1			1			2			11	
WOOD, Betty (c)								2		1		
WOOD, Edward (c)	1	1	1		1			2	1	1	2	
WOOD, Isaac (c)	1			1				1	1			
WOOD, Jesse (c)			2		1				1		1	
WOOD, John (c) (of James)		1							1			
WOOD, John (c)		1							1			
WOOD, John (c) (of John)	2			1		2			1		9	
WOOD, Jonathan (a)	2	1		2		2			1	1		
WOOD, Leonard (c)	2			1		1		1	1		1	
WOOD, Rebecca (a)	1					1		2		2		
WOOD, Richard (c)		2	1					1		1		
WOOD, Sabrit (c)			1		1						19	
WOOD, Samuel (a)					1	1	2		1	1	10	3
WOOD, Sue (a)	1					1		1				
WOOD, Thomas B. (a)				1					1			
WOOD, William (a)				1		1		1			18	2
WOOD, William (c)				1						1		

Head of the family	Free white males					Free white females					Other free persons	Number of slaves
	Under 10	10 - 16	16 - 26	26 - 45	Over 45	Under 10	10 - 16	16 - 26	26 - 45	Over 45		
WOODERD, Isaac (c)	2			1		1		1				
WOODFIELD, Joseph (a)	1	1	1	1				1				
WOOLF, Elias (c)	1	1		1			1		1		12	3
WOOLF, Samuel (c)	(blotted)				1			1			(blotted)	
WORTHY, Mary (a)	1							1				
YOC---, John (a)	2	2			1	2	1		4		13	
YOUNG, John (a)			2	1		1		2				
YOUNG, Thomas (a)		1	1	1				1	1		28	
YOUNG, William (a)	1			1				1	1	1		
YOUNGER, John (a)	6	2			1		1		1			
YOUNGER, Richard (a)	1	2		1		2			1		4	
YOUNGER, Richard, Jr.(a)				1				1				

CALVERT COUNTY, MARYLAND

1800 CENSUS

MARYLAND   GENEALOGICAL   SOCIETY,   INC.

T. Harvey Jones., Jr., President

128 Oakdale Avenue,   Baltimore, Maryland
21228

INTRODUCTION

Calvert County, Maryland is the smallest of the five southern counties. It was first mentioned when in July 1654, the Council decided, in accordance with the instructions received from the Lord Proprietor, to make both sides of the Patuxent River into one County. As originally established it took in an area much greater than at the present. It reached north to the headwaters of the Patuxent including some of what is now Howard County, much of what is known as Prince George's County and parts of Montgomery, as far north as the Great Falls on the Potomac River.

Maryland Geological Survey, by Wm. Bullock Clark and Edw. B. Mathews, Vol. VI, p. 454 describes it as:

"on the southside by Pynehill River or creek to the head thereof and from thence through the woods to the head of Patuxent River being the northerly bounds of St. Mary's County and bounded on the northside with the Creeke; on the western side of the Chesapeake Bay called Herring Creeke and from thence through the woods to the head of Patuxent River being the Southerly bound of Ann-arundell County."

Prior to 1654 there existed what is known as "Old Charles County." Old Charles County was of short duration. When erected by the Governor on Nov. 21, 1650, "Old Charles County" was on the south side of the Patuxent River and included what are now parts of St. Mary's, Charles and Prince George's counties. Md. Arch. 3:259. When Prince George's County was formed April 23, 1695 the parent counties from what it was formed were, Calvert and Charles. It was at this time, 1695 - 1696 that Calvert County lost much of its extensive territory. However, of counties erected during the seventeenth century, Calvert and Charles have suffered less changes and curtailment in their territorial limits. Present day Charles County was formed April 13, 1658. The present day northern boundary of Calvert County separating it from Anne Arundel County was established by law, Act of General Assembly 1822 and '23.

The first settlers of Calvert County are believed to have moved up an old Indian trail from St. Mary's City to a point on the Patuxent River. These were Jesuit Missionaries and established themselves at Mattapany about 10 miles north of the mouth of the river. This was about 1637. Records show another settlement as early as 1642 on St. Leonard's Creek.

With the passage of the Toleration Act, on or about April 21, 1649, quite a sizable group of Puritans from Virginia took up residence along the shores of Severn River. Soon they began to spread out into Calvert County. Some took lands in the region of the Cliffs as far south as Parker's Creek. Others settled in the lower part of the County.

Quakers began to locate in Calvert County soon after 1657 when three Quaker Missionaries came from Virginia into Maryland. Quakers established settlements on the lower and upper Cliffs at St. Leonard's and below Plum Point, respectively. George Fox visited Calvert County in 1672.

Many other of the early settlers of Calvert County belonged to the Church of England. To serve the central and lower part of the county, a small building was erected known as Christ Church about 1670. Not much later, All Saints Church was built in the upper part of the county.

The 1800 Census for Calvert County is divided into two areas or Parishes. Since the census is arranged alphabetically, the parish in which the person lived is designated by (a) "All Saints Parish" or (c) "Christ Church Parish." There are approximately 800 names in the 1800 Census of Calvert County.

References: Maryland Geological Survey, Vol. VI, pub. 1906, The Johns Hopkins Press.
A History of Calvert County Maryland, by Charles F. Stein, pub. 1960.

1800 CENSUS -- STATE OF MARYLAND

County: **CHARLES COUNTY**

District: **DURHAM PARISH**

Name	Males -10	10-16	16-26	26-45	+45	Females -10	10-16	16-26	26-45	+45	Free	Slaves	Total
(Name not decipherable - p. 493)						1			2			3	
........., John			1					1	1				
Adams, Charles	3		1			2	2		1			11	
Adams, John, Jr.	2		1	1		2			1	1		5	
Adams, Josias			1		1			2		1		4	
Adams, Lyddia		3	1							1		5	
Adams, Walter			2				1	1				3	
Adams, William	1			1					1				
Adams, William G.	2			1		2	2		1		1	18	
Allen, George	1	1				1		1		1			
Allen, John												1	
Allen, Levi	1			1				1	1			1	
Allen, William	2	1	1		1	2			1				
Anderson, George	1		1					1					
Anderson, Joseph	1		1			1		1					
Armstrong, Robert	2		1				1		1			3	
Baillie, Andrew						1	1					38	
Baker, Jane								1		1			
Baker, William		1		1				1				1	
Barker, Isaac				1				1	1				
Barker, Shadrach		1	2		1		1	2		1		1	
Barns, Richard, Sr.					1	1		1	1			23	
Barnes, Humphrey			2	1		1		1				14	
Barnes, Richard, Jr.			1	1								7	
Bastin, Matthew	3		2	1		1	1	1					
Bastin, William			1				1	1	1				
Bayne, William				1		2			1			6	
Bell, Godfrey	1	1		1		2			1				
Benson, Benjamin	2			1		2			1			14	
Berry, Benjamin	1		1					1				5	
Blandford, Joseph	2			1		1		1					
Bloxham, Abram	2	1						1					
Boswell, Charles	1	1		1					1			1	
Boswell, John	1			1				2				4	
Boswell, John	2			1		2			1			6	
Boswell, William		1	1	1		2	1	1				2	
Bowie, Abram				1									
Bowie, Elizabeth	1					1			1				
Bowie, Isaac			1	1		1		1					
Bowie, James P.			1		1	1	1	1					
Bowie, Mary Ann				1				3	1	1			
Bowie, Rhody	1	1	1		1		2	2			1	1	
Bowie, Theophilus		1		1				2	1			7	

1800 CENSUS -- STATE OF MARYLAND

County: **CHARLES COUNTY**

District: **DURHAM PARISH**

Name	Males -10	10-16	16-26	26-45	+45	Females -10	10-16	16-26	26-45	+45	Free	Slaves	Total
Bradley, John			1						1			1	
Bradshaw, Jeremiah	2		1	1		3	2		1				
Brawner, Barton		1	3	3	1		1	1		1	3	12	
Brawner, Benjamin			1		1			1		1		8	
Brawner, Edward	3	1	2	1		2	1	1				3	
Brawner, Isaac	1			1		2			1			5	
Brawner, John C.		2		1		3	1		1	1		7	
Brawner, Joseph	3	1		1		1		1				12	
Brawner, William, Jr.	3	1		1		1	1		1		1	3	
Brawner, William, Jr.			1		1							15	
Brooke, Walter D.			1					1				8	
Buchell, Charles		1	2		1	1		1		1	1	1	
Bullman, Thomas					1		1	2		1		4	
Burgess, Mary			2					1		1		4	
Bush, John, Jr.					1					1		9	
Bush, John, Jr.	1			1		1			2			6	
Butler, Eleanor											7		
Butler, Mary											10		
Carpenter, John	2		1		1	3			1			1	
Carpenter, Viney	1		1				1	2	1				
Carpenter, William		1			1	1			1			4	
Carroll, Elizabeth	1		1							1			
Carroll, Richard	1				1	2	1		2				
Cato, George		2	1		1	2	1		1			12	
Channing, Chloe	3							2	1				
Ching, Rosamond									1	1			
Clements, John	1		1			2		1	1		1	4	
Clements, Walter	1	3			1	1			1				
Clinkscales, Samuel				1				1		1		4	
Coby, John	1	1		1		1			2			12	
Coffer, Elizabeth	1	2	1			1	1			1		4	
Colvin, William			1		1					1			
Courts, John, Dr.	4	1	6	2		3			2	1		81	
Davis, Benjamin	1	2	2		1	2	1	1				9	
Davis, David	1	1		1		3	3		1				
Davis, Elizabeth			1	1	1			1	1	1		1	
Davis, James		1	1		1			2					
Davis, Jenefer	2			1		1		1					
Davis, Jeremiah			2		1			1		1			
Davis, Joseph				1					1				
Davis, Patience								1	1	1		1	
Davis, Richard	1	1			1		1	1		1			
Davis, Sarah	1								2			31	

1800 CENSUS -- STATE OF MARYLAND

County: **CHARLES COUNTY**

District: **DURHAM PARISH**

Name	Males -10	10-16	16-26	26-45	+45	Females -10	10-16	16-26	26-45	+45	Free	Slaves	Total
Deane, Charles	1		1			1		1					
Deane, Sally	1		1			1	1		1				
Delozier, John	2	2			1	1				1	1		
Delozier, Thomas			1		1			2		1		2	
Dent, William	2			1			1	2			1	29	
Donaldson, Ann	1								1				
Doyne, Ann	1		1					1	1			9	
Duffy, Moses	1		1				1	1	1				
Dunnington, Francis	3	2		1	2			3	2			20	
Dunnington, George			1		1			1	2	1	1	17	
Dunnington, James			1	1	1	1		2	1			12	
Dunnington, Peter, Sr.		1		1	1			2		1		1	
Dunnington, Peter, Jr.	4			1				1				1	
Dunnington, William	2		1		1			1	1	1		3	
Dyall, Catherine		1	2			1	1	1		1		1	
Elgin, Francis	3		1	1									
Elgin, Hezekiah				1		3			1			5	
Elgin, Joseph	3		1	1		2			1	1		18	
Elliot, Thomas	1			1				1		1			
Essex, a free Negro											2	1	
Evans, Levi	1	1		1				2		1		5	
Ferrel, Elisha	2		1		1	1			1			2	
Ferrell, James	3	1	1		1	1	1	1	1	1			
Fewell, John			1			1	1	1					
Flannagin, Ann	1						1		1				
Flewry, Edward		1	1		1			1	1			5	
Flowers, Elizabeth		1	1					1	1	1	1		
Ford, George N.	1			1					1			10	
Fowke, Margery		1	1			1	1		1			42	
Fowke, Roger		2		1								13	
Fowler, William	1		1					1				1	
Franklin, Edward	2	2		1		2			1	1		37	
Franklin, Francis			2						1			8	
Franklin, Hezekiah			1	1	1		2	2		1		8	
Franklin, James	1	1		1		2	1		1	1	1	8	
Franklin, Nehemiah				1								3	
Franklin, William	1	1		1		2	1	1		1		6	
Franklin, William R.	2		1	1		1	1		2				
Franklin, Zephaniah				1	1							14	
Frawner, Ann			1	1			1			2			

1800 CENSUS -- STATE OF MARYLAND

County: CHARLES COUNTY

District: DURHAM PARISH

Name	M -10	M 10-16	M 16-26	M 26-45	M +45	F -10	F 10-16	F 16-26	F 26-45	F +45	Free	Slaves	Total
Garner, Mary			2		,	1	1	1					
Garner, Theophilus				1		1			1			26	
Garnor, Hezekiah	4	2		1				1	1	1	1	11	
Gaskin, Richard				1								1	
Gilbert, Joseph		1			1	2	1		1		1		
Golden, Robert	1	1	1		1	2			2				
Gray, Andrew	1	2			1	1			1				
Gray, George	1		1	1		2	1		1			2	
Gray, Hannah	1			1		1			1	1		17	
Gray, Jahzeel	1			1		2			1			8	
Gray, Jeremiah			1		1			1		1		9	
Gray, John F.			1	2								10	
Gray, John N.						2		1				6	
Gray, Joseph	1	2				1	1	1	1	1		15	
Gray, Wilson	1	1				1	1		1				
Green, John	1		1						1	1			
Green, Samuel			1			4	1		1				
Green, Sarah						2			1			4	
Griffin, John	2			1		2	1	1			3	1	
Griffin, Thomas			1			3		1	1				
Griffin, William	3			1					1			1	
Groves, Abednego	2		1	2		2		2					
Groves, John	1	1	1		1	1	2	3	1				
Groves, William	1		1		1	2	1		1				
Haislope, John (of Henry)			3		1	1	2	1	1	1		1	
Haislope, Samuel		2	1		-			1	1	1		12	
Hales, Catherine	1					1	1		1				
Hall, Jane											7		
Hall, John	1				1	1			1			2	
Hamilton, Eleanor A.	1							1	2	1		8	
Hamilton, Elizabeth								1	1				
Hanson, Samuel, Dr.	2	1		1		2			2			12	
Hanson, Samuel (of Wm.)	1				1	2		1	1	1		15	
Harrison, William		1	1					3			1	20	
Hart, Catherine	1					3		1	1				
Hatcher, Ignatius	1		1	1		2	1		1		1	1	
Heifler, John			2		1				1	1	1	1	
Hewes, Ralph			3	2	1				1			38	
Hewlett, William	2		2	2	1	2		1				44	
Highfields, Frederick	1		1	1		1			1				
Howard, John	1	1			1	2	2		1				
Hudson, George				1		3			1	1	2	21	
Hudson, Tabitha			1						1			2	
Hurley, Sarah			1							1			
Hutchison, John	2		1			2	1	1	1			1	

1800 CENSUS -- STATE OF MARYLAND

County: **CHARLES COUNTY**

District: **DURHAM PARISH**

Name	\-10	10-16	16-26	26-45	+45	\-10	10-16	16-26	26-45	+45	Free	Slaves	Total
	Males					Females							
Jackson, Thomas	2		1		1		1	1		1		4	
Jackson, William											6		
Jenkins, Elizabeth						1	1		1				
Jenkins, Ephraim	1			1						1			
Jenkins, Levi	4			1		1	1		1				
Jenkins, Wilson	2	1	1	1		2		1		1			
Johnson, Lawson	1			1		2			1				
Jones, Elizabeth	1	1							1				
Jones, John C.	1			2		3			1		1	19	
Jones, Mary S.	1	2	2	1				1	2	1		37	
Jones, Samuel			1	1		1			1			26	
Jones, William	1		1	1					2			1	
Keibeard, Thomas			1		1	1		2	1			4	
Kennedy Clement			2	1	1	1	2	1				20	
Kennedy, William	3	1		1	1	2	2		1			2	
King, Charles	1			1		3	1		1	1			
Langley, John				1		1		1				7	
Lewis, George				1		1			2				
Linkins, Eleanor	1	1						1		1			
Linkins, Sarah											7		
Lloyd, Mendkin	3		1	1		1			1			3	
Lomax, John	1		1		1			2		1		1	
Love, Leonard	2		1			2	2		1			1	
Love, Samuel				?			2			1			
Luckett, Margaret			1					1		1		10	
Luckett, Samuel		1			1			2				1	
Lyles, George N.	2		1			2			1			18	
Lynch, Daniel	1				1			1					
McBayne, Ignatius	1		1			1	1	1				2	
McBayne, John	1			1				1				3	
McBayne, William		1			1			3		1		5	
McBayne, William, Jr.		1		1		2		2				1	
McConchie, William, Jr.	1			2		3			1			18	
McCoy, Johnson		2			1	1	1	1	1	1		5	
McDonald, Patrick						1						4	
McDonald, Zachariah			1	1	1				2			14	
McPherson, John	3			1		2	2		1			13	
McPherson, Saml, Major				1	1				1			14	
Maddox, Mary		1	2					2	1	1			
Maddox, Nancy										1			
Maddox, Rhoda			2		1	2	1	1				2	

1800 CENSUS -- STATE OF MARYLAND

County: **CHARLES COUNTY**

District: **DURHAM PARISH**

Name	Males					Females					Free	Slaves	Total
	-10	10-16	16-26	26-45	+45	-10	10-16	16-26	26-45	+45			
Mahew, Catherine			1					2	1	1			5
Mankin, Joseph				1						1			
Marr, Daniel		2	2		1	1		1	1				
Marr, John	1	1	1		1	3	2		1				
Martin, Allen	3	2		2		1			1				4
Martin, Elias				1		3	1		1				
Martin, Elijah	3	2		1		1							2
Mason, Lott	1				1		2		1	1			6
May, William					1		1	2		1			1
Meeke, John B.			1	2	1			1		1			26
Meeke, Thomas				1			1	1	1				6
Middleton, Samuel		1		1		4		1	1				33
Milstead, Barton	1			1				1					5
Milstead, Elizabeth		1	1				1			1			
Milstead, Isaac				1		1		1					1
Milstead, John B.				1					1				7
Milstead, Matthew		1			1			2	1				
Milstead, Samuel	1	1		1	1		2	2		1			6
Milstead, Thomas	2	1		1		3		2	1				2
Milstead, Walter	2			1					1				1
Milstead, William					1				1	1			8
Mitchell, John, Gen.	2	1		2		2			1				24
Morris, James	1			1		2	2		1				13
Muncaster, James		1			1		1	1					14
Murdock, Edward				1				1	1				1
Murdock, Godfrey			1		1			2	1	1			6
Murdock, James	1	1			1			2	1				
Murdock, Jane		1	2					1	1	1			
Murdock, Levi				1							4	1	
Murdock, William			1		1			2		1			1
Muschett, Mungo	3	1		1			1		1				15
Naile, Charles				1		1			1				
Naile, Elizabeth						1			1	1			
Nalley, John					1			1	1				
Nalley, Richard	2	1	1		1	1	2		1				8
Neale, Walter				1		2		1					2
Nelson, Frederick	3	3		2					1				
Nelson, John				1			1		1				4
Nelson, Thomas of Thos.	1	2	1	1		3		2	2	1			11
Norris, Daniel	4	1			1				1				12
Parsons, Thomas	1			1					1				
Perry, John	1			1	1	2			1				9
Perry, Robert	2	1		1		1		1					5
Perry, Thomas	1			1	1			1					11

1800 CENSUS -- STATE OF MARYLAND

County: **CHARLES COUNTY**

District: **DURHAM PARISH**

Name	Males -10	10-16	16-26	26-45	+45	Females -10	10-16	16-26	26-45	+45	Free	Slaves	Total
Picken, John		1	1		1	1	1		1				
Posey, Ann				1		1			1	1			
Posey, Anthony	1		1					1				1	
Posey, Burdet	2	1	2		1	1	1	1	1			3	
Posey, Henry	1			1		2	1		1			13	
Posey, Humphrey		1			1	3	1	2				8	
Posey, James				1		3			1			15	
Posey, Jeremiah		1			1	2	1	1	1				
Posey, Jessee	1			1		3			2				
Posey, Joseph H.	1			1		2			1			5	
Posey, Rhoda	1		1		1		1	1	1				
Posey, Roger	3		2	1					1				
Posey, Thomas			1		1		1		1				
Posey, Uzziah			1		1				1			8	
Posey, William	2	1	1		1		1		1		2		
Price, Joseph	2							2				6	
Price, Richard	1		4	2		1		1				10	
Price, Thomas	1	1	1	1		3			2			5	
Price, Zachariah	1			1		1	1		1			19	
Ratleff, Joseph, Sr.	1	2			1	2			1	1			
Ratleff, William				1		1			1			3	
Ratliff, Ignatius			4	2	1			1		1		5	
Ratliff, Joseph, Jr.	1			1		1	1	2				2	
Ratliff, Rhody		1	1		1	1	1	1		1		2	
Rice, James	2					1			1				
Richardson, Luke	1	1		1		1			1			1	
Rizen, Ann		1	1					1		1		5	
Rizen, Chandler	2	2			1			2					
Rizen, Peter			2										
Rizen, Philip	2	1		1		1	2					4	
Robertson, John	2			1								26	
Robertson, Maryann	1					1		1					
Robertson, William G.	1	2			1			2	1	1			
Ryan, Ignatius					1		2			2		45	
Rye, David	2	2		1		2		2	1				
Rye, John	2		1		1	3		3	1			1	
Rye, Warren	3	2			1	2		2		1		3	
Scott, James	2	2	3		1			1		1			
Shaw, William			1	1	1		2	2		1		19	
Shepard, Francis		1			1			2				4	
Shepherd, Thomas	1				1	3	1		1			4	
Shields, James	1	1	1				1	1		1		1	

1800 CENSUS -- STATE OF MARYLAND

County: **CHARLES COUNTY**

District: **DURHAM PARISH**

Name	\-10	10-16	16-26	26-45	+45	\-10	10-16	16-26	26-45	+45	Free	Slaves	Total
	Males					**Females**							
Simmes, Joseph	3	1	2		1	1	1		1	1		12	
Simmes, Massey	1		1	1		1		1				5	
Simmons, Aaron	3				1	3	2	1	1			2	
Simmons, John F.				1								12	
Simpson, John			1					1					
Skinner, Ann	1	1	1					1					
Skinner, Elisha	1			1		1		1	1			2	
Skinner, Ewell	2			1		1		1					
Skinner, Hezekiah			1		1	1	1			1			
Skinner, James	1			1	1	1		1		1		12	
Skinner, Jesse	2	1		1			1		1				
Skinner, John			2		1		1	1				9	
Skinner, John			2		1			2	1				
Skinner, Mary	3		1			3			2	1		7	
Skinner, Sarah		1	1							1			
Skinner, Walter		1		1		3			1			1	
Smallwood, Hezekiah	3	1		1		2	2		1			1	
Smallwood, Mary				2			1	2	1	1	1	2	
Smith, Benjamin				1		2	1		1				
Smith, Elizabeth								1		1		5	
Smith, John	2	1			1	2			1			4	
Smith, Roger, a free Black & Family											6		
Speake, Eleanor		1		1			2	1		1		9	
Speake, Francis	1	1	1		2		1	1				22	
Speake, Lawson	1	2		1		3			1			13	
Speake, Samuel	1	1		1				1				13	
Speake, Thomas I.	1		2	1				1				21	
Stewart, John	2			1		1	2		1				
Stewart, Nehemiah	2		2			1		1	1			3	
Stoddert, Sally		1		1					2			22	
Stone, Mary			1			2			3	1			
Stone, Thomas		1		1		1				1		6	
Sutherland, Ignatius		1	1			1	1		1				
Sutherland, James			1	1				1				1	
Sutherland, Walter	2		1			1			2			3	
Swann, Mary											9		
Tallmash, Mary	1		2	1		1	2	1			1		
Tallmash, William	2		1			1		1				1	
Taylor, Robert				1		2	1	2	1			17	
Taylor, Sarah		1	1					1	1				
Taylor, Sarah								1					
Thomas, Ann	1					1		2				23	
Thomas, Clement	3	2	1		1	1		1	1			2	
Thompson, Alexander	2		1			1			1	1			
Thompson, James	1		1			1		1					

1800 CENSUS -- STATE OF MARYLAND

County: __CHARLES COUNTY__

District: __DURHAM PARISH__

Name	\<Males\> -10	10-16	16-26	26-45	+45	\<Females\> -10	10-16	16-26	26-45	+45	Free	Slaves	Total
Thompson, John			1					1					
Thompson, Joseph				1		2		1	1			3	
Thompson, Leonard			1	1				2		1		1	
Thompson, Thomas	1		1		1			2		2		5	
Thompson, William				1		1		1	1				
Wapole, Avery	1			2				1					
Wapole, Gerard			1					1					
Wapole, James	1		1					3					
Wapole, John					1	1	2	1		1			
Ward, George	2											3	
Ward, Ignatius			2			1	1		2		1	6	
Ward, Susanna			1					1	1			3	
Warden, Ann			1							1		9	
West, Ann	1						2	1		1			
Wheeler, Ignatus M.				1				2		1		4	
Wheeler, Richard	1			1		3				1	1	11	
Whiting, Joan	1			1		3	1			1		3	
Wilford, Thirza	1					2				3			
Williams, John	2		1	1			3				1	10	
Wilson, Samuel	1		1	1				2				15	
Winter, Walter			1		1	1		1				8	
Woodward, Ann		1				1		1				2	
Wright, Gowry			1										
Wright, Lyddia									2				
Wright, Margaret				2		2		1	1			3	
Yates, Josias			1	1	1			1				7	
Young, Joseph	2	1	1					2	1			18	

1800 CENSUS -- STATE OF MARYLAND

County: __CHARLES COUNTY__

District: __PORT TOBACCO PARISH__

Name	Males -10	10-16	16-26	26-45	+45	Females -10	10-16	16-26	26-45	+45	Free	Slaves	Total
Acton, George	2		1						1				
Acton, Henry	1					2		1					
Acton, Henry, Sr.		1	1			1	1	1	2		1		
Acton, James						1		1			1		
Acton, John, Sr.						1	2		1			4	
Acton, Ozborn	2					1	1		1			5	
Acton, Theodore	1		1						1				
Acton, William				1		2			1				
Adams, Adam											2		
Adams, Benjamin	1			1		5			1				
Adams, Ignatius			1	2	1				1	1		9	
Adams, Jane											3		
Adams, Leonard				1				1		1		2	
Adams, Martin	1			1				1				1	
Adams, Richard	1		1		1			2				8	
Adams, William				2								4	
Arvin, Edward. D.	3	2		1				2	1	1			
Arvin, Thomas		1				1		1		1		1	
Arvin, Thomas	3	3				1	1		1				
Atchison, Joshua	3	1				1	1		1				
Athey, Charles	2	2		1		2	1		1	1			
Athey, Hezekiah						1						4	
Baker, William		1	2		1				1			2	
Barnes, Godshall	2	1		1		1			1			4	
Barnes, John H.	2			2		1		1				2	
Barnes, Thomas			1	1					1	1		6	
Barnes, William, Sr.				4		1	1	1	1	1	1		
Bateman, Alexander	3	1		1					1				
Bateman, Alexander	3			1					1				
Bateman, Benjamin		1				1		1	1	1			
Bealle, Ann								1	1			1	
Bealle, Benjamin			1			2		1				11	
Bealle, John F.	1	1		1		2			1			13	
Bealle, Penelope			1			1	1	1	1			12	
Beane, Benjamin	2			1		1			1			3	
Beane, Henry H.	4	2			1	1		3	1			1	
Beaven, William	2	1		1		1		2	1			2	
Bennett, Clare										1		1	
Berry, A. Samuel				2								20	
Berry, Benjamin, Sr.	1	1		2	1	1	1	3		1		3	
Berry, Henry						1	1		1		1	8	
Berry, Hezekiah		1				1		1			1	8	
Berry, Hezikiah	1			2		2			1			1	
Berry, Joseph						1			1	1	1	1	
Berry, Prior	2	1		1		2			1				
Berry, Samuel	1	1	3			1			2	1		3	

1800 CENSUS -- STATE OF MARYLAND

County: CHARLES COUNTY

District: PORT TOBACCO PARISH

Name	Males -10	10-16	16-26	26-45	+45	Females -10	10-16	16-26	26-45	+45	Free	Slaves	Total
Blackistone, Thomas			1										1
Blandford, Benjamin		1	1						1				3
Blandford, Nicholas	1		1			1							3
Blandford, Richard	3			1		1	1		1				2
Boarman, Benedict	2		1			2			1				9
Boone, Edward	2	1	2	1	1			1	2				16
Boone, John	1	1	1			1	2	1	1				7
Boswell, Alexander			1			3		1					1
Boswell, Elizah		1			1	4	1			1			7
Boswell, Ignatius	1	2	1			4			1				9
Boswell, John	4	2	1		1	1	1		1				19
Boswell, Joseph					1	1	2	1	1				1
Boswell, Matthew			1			1	1						2
Boswell, Rhoda			1										1
Boswell, Terry											6		
Boswell, Thomas	1		1			2	1		1				8
Boswell, Walter		1	1			2	1		1				3
Bowles, John		1	1				2	1		1			2
Bradley, Charles			1	1				1					3
Brandt, Jacob			1	1				1					1
Brent, John	1			2		1			1				59
Brent, Robert		2		1			1		1		1		25
Brent, William	1	1	3			2	1	1		1	1		21
Briscoe, Richard S.			1			2			1				12
Brooke, Baker					1								8
Brown, Gustavus R.		2			1	1	1	1	1				35
Burgess, Thomas	1		1			1	1	2					17
Burnwell, John	1	1	1			1	1						
Burroughs, John	1				1	3	1	1	3				
Burroughs, Samuel			1			3			1		3		2
Butler, Catherine											8		4
Butler, Henry													
Butler, Levi	1		1			1		1					2
Butler, Mary Ann	1	1	1	1				1	1				5
Cahooe, James	1	1	1			1		2		1			
Canter, Isaac		1	1			1	2	2		1			
Carnes, Margaret								1		1			
Carricoe, Monica								2		1			
Carrington, Daniel	2			1		1	1	1					4
Carrington, Susanna		1				1		1		1			3
Carrington, Timothy	1	1		1		1		1					8
Causin, Gerard. B.			1		1	1			1	1			50
Cawood, Benjamin	4	2				1	4		1	1			32
Chandler, John	1	1	1			1	1		1				6

1800 CENSUS -- STATE OF MARYLAND

County: CHARLES COUNTY

District: PORT TOBACCO PARISH

Name	Males					Females					Free	Slaves	Total
	-10	10-16	16-26	26-45	+45	-10	10-16	16-26	26-45	+45			
Chandler, Samuel				1						1		7	
Chandler, Stephen				1		2			1		1	1	
Chapman, Henry H.			1	1		1		1				18	
Chapman, John					1				1	1		32	
Chapman, Samuel	1	2		2		1		1				49	
Clements, Abednego	2			2			1	1	1				
Clements, David				1		1			1			1	
Clements, John A.	2				1	1	1	2	2				
Clements, John of Frs.						1		2				27	
Clements, John F.	1			1		2	1	1					
Clements, Leonard	1	2		1		1	1		1			9	
Clements, Mary		1		1				1	1	1		12	
Clements, Mary Ann	1	1		1		2	2	1	1			1	
Clements, Matthias				1								1	
Clements, Samuel			2			1			2	1			
Clements, Thomas				1		1			1				
Clements, Walter	4					1		2	1			8	
Clements, William						1		1	1				
Clements, William		1		1		1		1	1			6	
Clinkscales, Jane								1	1	1	1	1	
Colley, James	1					1					1		
Cook, William		2	2	2		2		1			1	16	
Cooksey, Hezekiah	2		2	2		1	2	1				14	
Coomes, Charles		1		1		2		1				8	
Coomes, Clare	1					2	2		1			7	
Coomes, Jane				1		2	3	1				4	
Coomes, Sarah			2					1	2	1			
Coomes, Teresa	3	1				1		1	1			20	
Coomes, Thomas W.					1					1		12	
Cooper, James	3			1		2			1			3	
Courts, Charles	1	1	1		1		1	3	1				
Cox, Charles				1		1			2	2			
Cox, Francis	1			1			1		1			2	
Cox, Samuel	1	2		1	1	2		4		1		23	
Cox, William, Senr.			1	1	1				1			10	
Cox, William, Jr.				1					1				
Crackles, Mary			1	1				1		1		7	
Crismond, Aaron						1	1		1	1	1		
Crismond, Mary	1	1		1				1		1		2	
Curtis, Mary											2		
Dagg, John			3	1			1				1	2	
Daniel, John M.	1			1		3			1			9	
Davidson, Henry			1	1		3			1			10	

1800 CENSUS -- STATE OF MARYLAND

County: **CHARLES COUNTY**

District: **PORT TOBACCO PARISH**

Name	\-10	10-16	16-26	26-45	+45	\-10	10-16	16-26	26-45	+45	Free	Slaves	Total
	Males					Females							
Davis, Cornelius			3						1		1		
Davis, Hendley	1		2						1	1			
Davis, Mary						1		1		1			
Deakins, Edward			2		1		2	3		1		7	
Deakins, Francis				1			2		1			1	
Dent, Henry of Thos.		1	1	1								2	
Digges, Jane			3						1			37	
Dixon, Edward			1					1				1	
Dixon, Francis		1	1		1	2		1		1			
Dixon, Leonard	2		1			2			1	1			
Dodson, Ann			2					1		1	1	5	
Dodson, Ignatius	2		1	1		3			1			8	
Dodson, John				1					1			2	
Dodson, Lyddia								1	2	1		14	
Dodson, William B.	1	2	1		1	3	1	1	1				
Douglass, Chloe	1	1						2		1		9	
Downing, Butler	5	1		1		1	1		1				
Downs, William	2	1		1		2			1			7	
Duckett, John B.			1								1	2	
Dulaney, Benjamin	2			1				1	1			32	
Dunbox, William	1			1		1			1				
Dyer, Jeremiah	4	1		1		1	1	2	1			10	
Dyson, John			1	1		1		1			1	8	
Dyson, Thomas A.			1	1	2	1	1	1	1			28	
Edelin, Basil	3	1		1			1		1			7	
Edelin, Francis				1			1	1	1			4	
Edelin, George	4			1		1			1			5	
Edelin, John	1			1		1	3		1	1		1	
Fenwick, Ann	4			1					1			20	
Ferguson, Robert				2	1				1			15	
Fitzgerald, Thomas	2			1					1			1	
Ford, Ann								1		1		14	
Ford, J. Philip				2						1		19	
Ford, John E.				2								1	
Ford, William Penn				1								5	
Frazier, Daniel			1								1		
Freeman, Benjamin	2			1					1			1	
Freeman, Nathaniel	2			1	1	2	2		1			55	
Freeman, Nathaniel, Jr.		1		1								1	
Gambria, Sarah			2	1					1			18	
Garner, Charles					1		1				1	11	

1800 CENSUS -- STATE OF MARYLAND

County: CHARLES COUNTY

District: PORT TOBACCO PARISH

Name	\-10 (M)	10-16 (M)	16-26 (M)	26-45 (M)	+45 (M)	\-10 (F)	10-16 (F)	16-26 (F)	26-45 (F)	+45 (F)	Free	Slaves	Total
Garner, John					1	1	2	2		1		2	
Garner, Matthew				1								5	
Gates, James	1		2	1		1		1	1			1	
Gates, James, Sr.	1	1	1		1	1	1		1			1	
Gibbons, Benjamin			2					1	1				
Gibson, John, Jr.			1			1		2			3	1	
Godfrey, Eleanor									1		3		
Graham, James		1		3					1		1	4	
Gray, Walter				1				1				2	
Green, Charles			1		1					1		13	
Green, Giles				1	1							12	
Green, Henry, Sr.			2		1	2		2		1		13	
Green, Henry, Jr.			1		1	1	1	1				7	
Green, John				1	1		1	1		1	2	1	
Green, Joseph	2			1		2			1		1	15	
Green, Melchizedeck			1		1	2	2	2		1			
Green, Nicholas			1	1			1		3			2	
Green, Wilford			1	2			1					8	
Green, William				1			1	1	1	1			
Green, Zachariah	2			1		2			1			6	
Greer, Ann	1	1				1	1		1				
Griffin, Ann			1					3	1	1		4	
Griffin, John		1	1		1			1	1	1		2	
Griffin, Joseph											2		
Griffin, William S.	1	1		1		3			1				
Guest, Robert		1	1	1								2	
Guy, William, Jr.	2			1		3						3	
Hagan, Basel	3			1	1	4			1		1		
Hagan, John	3			1					1			5	
Hagan, Joseph	2		1	1				1		1		10	
Hagan, Monica	1	1	1							1		14	
Haislope, John of Robt.	1		1		1	2	2		1			11	
Hall, Bridget											5		
Hamilton, Alexander		2		1					1	1			
Hamilton, Bennett		1	1		1		1	2		1		13	
Hamilton, Edward	1			1		2		1				19	
Hamilton, Priscilla	1	1	2	1		1			1				
Hamilton, Rhodias	1			1		3		1					
Hamilton, Samuel	2	1	1	1	1	2		3		1		33	
Hamilton, William			1	1				1		1		10	
Hammett, Peter											12		
Hannon, Henry	1	2		1		2	1		1				
Hannon, Walter W.	4			1					1			4	
Hanson, Catherine Q.								1		1		7	

1800 CENSUS -- STATE OF MARYLAND

County: __CHARLES COUNTY__

District: __PORT TOBACCO PARISH__

Name	Males -10	10-16	16-26	26-45	+45	Females -10	10-16	16-26	26-45	+45	Free	Slaves	Total
Hanson, Henry M.	1				1	3		1	1			9	
Hanson, John B.		1				1		1					
Hanson, Samuel, Sr.			1		1	1		1	2	1		36	
Hanson, Samuel of Walter	2	1	1	1		2	1		1			11	
Hanson, Sarah						1			1	1		19	
Hanson, Theophilus				2	1	1			1	1		25	
Hargraves, George			1			1		1	2			14	
Hawkins, Caleb, Esqr.			1	1								16	
Hawkins, Francis W.	2			1		1			1			36	
Hawkins, Henry H.	1			1					1			15	
Hawkins, Jane	1			1					1	2		21	
Hawkins, Samuel	1			1					2			24	
Hawkins, Smith	1	1		1		1	2	1		1		52	
Hay, William				1				2				4	
Hayden, Bernard				1		1			1				
Hays, Rebecca		1						1				6	
Hays, Thomas	3	2			1	1		2				4	
Hays, William	2	1			1	1	2		1				
Herbert, James			1		1		1			1		6	
Hide, George	3	1			1	2	2		1				
Hill, Charity											3	2	
Hill, Charity											3		
Hill, Samuel	1			1		1	1						
Hill, William											6		
Holden, James	1				1	2			1	1		3	
Hopewell, Clare G.	2	2	1			1	1		1		1	8	
Horrell, Dorothy		1	3						1			4	
Howard, Thomas G.	1	1	1		1		1	1		1		4	
Howard, William			2	1				2				4	
Howell, John			1									1	
Hunt, Jonathan		1		1	1			3		1			
Hunt, Joseph	2	2	1		1			2		1		1	
Hunt, Sylvester	2	2		1		1			1				
Hunt, William	2			1		1		1				2	
Hurry, John	1	1			1	1	1	1				6	
Jackson, William											6		
Jameson, Benjamin			1		1							12	
Jameson, Leonard					1			2	1			4	
Jenifer, Daniel	2	1			1	1						8	
Jenkins, George		1		1		2	1		1	1		47	
Jenkins, William	2	1	1	1		2	2	1	1	1			
Johnson, Andrew	2		1			2		3				1	
Johnson, Ann		1	1			1			2			2	

1800 CENSUS -- STATE OF MARYLAND

County: __CHARLES COUNTY__

District: __PORT TOBACCO PARISH__

| | Males | | | | | Females | | | | | | | |
Name	-10	10-16	16-26	26-45	+45	-10	10-16	16-26	26-45	+45	Free	Slaves	Total
Johnson, Archibald	2		1			1		1		1	1	9	
Johnson, Elisabeth		1					1	1		1		5	
Johnson, Hezekiah		1		1		1		2				9	
Johnson, Marshall	1		1					1				5	
Keech, John			1								1	8	
Kennyman, Parker	2		1				1			1			
Kerrick, Edward				1							1	3	
King, Ann	1							1	2			8	
King, John B.	3	1		1		3		1				9	
King, William		2		1		4		1	1			5	
Kitchen, William					1		1			1			
Knott, Joseph		1		1				1				1	
Knott, Justinian	1		1		1	2	1	1		1		5	
Lemmon, Charles S.		1		1		1	2	1	1				
Langley, John F.	1	2	1	1				2	1	1			
Langley, Thomas	1		1					1				1	
Langley, William		2		1				1		1			
Langley, William, Jr.			1			2			1			1	
Langloy, William, Sr.		1	1	1		1				1			
Lansberrie, Samuel	2	1	1					3	1	1		18	
Latimer, James	2			1		1			1			7	
Latimer, Judith			1							1		14	
Lawson, Michael			1			3			1			1	
Layman, Ann	2							2				1	
Layman, John C.	1			3		1	1	1	1	1	1	4	
Lee, George						1	1		2			27	
Leigh, William						1			1			5	
Lemaster, Eleanor							1	1	1				
Lindsey, Jane		2		1				3	1	1			
Linkins, Peter											5		
Lomax, Benjamin	1	2		1	1		1	1		1			
Lomax, John			1			1			1				
Lomax, Nelley											3		
Lovelace, William	1	1		1		2	1		1			1	
Lovelin, William	1			1		1			1			1	
Lucas, George			1	1								2	
Lucas, John R.	1			1		1			1				
Luckett, Ignatius			1	1						1		11	
Luckett, Jane		1				1		1		1			
Luckett, Joseph			1	1					3			29	

1800 CENSUS -- STATE OF MARYLAND

County: CHARLES COUNTY

District: PORT TOBACCO PARISH

Name	Males -10	10-16	16-26	26-45	+45	Females -10	10-16	16-26	26-45	+45	Free	Slaves	Total
McAtee, Benjamin				1					1				5
McConchie, William, Sr.	2		1	1	1		2			1			29
McDaniel, Allen	2				1	2	3				1		6
McDaniel, Archibald	1			1					1	1			1
McDaniel, Benedicta	1	1	2			2	1		4	1			3
McDaniel, Isaac				1						1			3
McDaniel, Jonathan	1	1			1	1		2		1			
McDaniel, Nathan	3			1		1	1		1				
McDaniel, Theophilus	2			1		2			1		1		1
McDonough, Maurice Jas.					1					1			8
McPherson, Catharine G.		2	2						1				6
McPherson, Elizabeth	1					2			1				10
McPherson, Elizabeth						3	3	1		1			19
McPherson, William, Sr.		3			1	1	1	1	2				25
McPherson, William H.	1		1	1	1	2	1		1				21
Maddocke, Henry					1		2						1
Maddox, Joseph	1			1				1					5
Maddox, Notley	1			1		1		1			1		
Maddox, Sarah		1							2				1
Maddox, Townly				1		2	1		1				1
Mahorney, Basel		1			1	1			1				2
Mahorney, Ignatius	1				1	1		1					
Mankin, Charles					1	1	1	1					10
Mankin, Richard T.	1			1			2			1			4
Mannary, Sarah		2	1		1	1	1			1			1
Manning, Francis	1			1	1	1	1	1				14
Marbury, Joseph			1	1									5
Marlow, Butler				1		1	1		1				2
Marlow, Richard	1		1		1		1	2		1			1
Marlow, Samuel	1		1		1			1					1
Marshall, John (of Philip)			1					1					
Marshall, Philip					1			2			1		20
Marshall, Samuel					1	1		2					10
Marshall, William		2			1		1	2		1			4
Martin, Henry	3		1					1	1				1
Martin, Michael	1		2		1	3	2	2	1		1		7
Martin, Thomas					1	1				1			9
Mason, William	2			1	1				1				46
Matthews, Ignatius					1		1	1					6
Matthews, Luke F.	1		1	1	1		1		1				35
Meekum, Samuel	2			1		1		1	1				1
Middleton, Ignatius			1	3					1				18
Middleton, Isaac					1	2			1				
Middleton, James	4		1	1		3			2				21
Miles, Edward	1			1	1	1		1	1	1			10
Miles, Edward L.		1	6	1		1		1					3

1800 CENSUS -- STATE OF MARYLAND

County: __CHARLES COUNTY__

District: __PORT TOBACCO PARISH__

Name	Males -10	10-16	16-26	26-45	+45	Females -10	10-16	16-26	26-45	+45	Free	Slaves	Total
Miles, Henry	1	2			1		1	1		1		5	
Miles, Nicholas			2	1								3	
Miles, Peter			4									1	
Millar, Winefred						2	1		1				
Mills, John B., Sr.		1	2		1		1	2				12	
Mitchell, Richard				1		2			1			7	
Mitchell, Richard B.	1	1		1			2		1	1		34	
Monroe, Alexander	1			1		2			1			1	
Monroe, Thomas, Jr.	1			1		1	1		1				
Montgomery, Henry	1			1				1				2	
Montgomery, James		1	1		1	3	1			1		1	
Montgomery, Joshua	1			1		1	2	3		1		3	
Moore, Elizah	2		1		1	1	2	1				1	
Moore, Henry	5		1	1			1		1			1	
Moore, James					1					1		14	
Moore, Matthew	1		1		1		1	2					
Moore, Matthew, Sr.			1		1			1		1		8	
Moran, Gabriel					1	2			1			8	
Moreland, Eleanor	1	1				2	2			1			
Moreland, James	1			1					1				
Moreland, James	3	1			1	2	1	2	1			2	
Moreland, Joseph	3			1		2	1		1			2	
Moreland, Patrick					1				1			2	
Moreland, Philip	2	2		1		2		1	1				
Moreland, Philip, Jr.			1	1								2	
Moreland, Richard					1					2		15	
Moreland, Samuel	1	1		1		1	1		1				
Moreland, Sarah			1							1			
Moreland, Stephen	2		2		1	2	1	2	1				
Moreland, William	2		3	2	1					1		5	
Moreland, William	2			1		3			1				
Moreland, Zachariah				1			1	2	1				
Morrison, William	1				1		2	1	1				
Morriss, Jacob				1	1				1			10	
Morriss, Robert		1	1	1								1	
Morriss, Walter			1		1							3	
Morriss, William	1	1	1	1			2	1	1			17	
Mudd, Ann	1	1				2	1		2				
Mudd, Jeremiah			2	1				1				7	
Mudd, Joseph		1			1				1			17	
Mudd, Joshua	3	2	2		2	2	1			1		18	
Mudd, Leonard				1				2				7	
Mudd, Lucy		1						3			2		
Mudd, Susanna		1		1		3	2	1	1			7	
Murdock, William	3			1		1			1		1	32	
Murray, Hugh	1		2	1		1		1				3	
Murray, John			2					1				1	
Murray, Nicholas			1	1								1	

1800 CENSUS -- STATE OF MARYLAND

County: __CHARLES COUNTY__

District: __PORT TOBACCO PARISH__

Name	Males -10	10-16	16-26	26-45	+45	Females -10	10-16	16-26	26-45	+45	Free	Slaves	Total
Nalley, James			1			1		1					
Nalley, Susanna				2	3	1	1	3	2	1			
Nalley, Thomas				2		1	1	2		1			8
Neale, Charles, Rev d,(in the Monastery)					1	1		10	5	3	2	20	
Neale, Edward		2	1	1		2		1					14
Neale, Henry		3											2
Neale, Joseph	1		1	1		1	1	2					6
Nelson, Joseph	1					1	2	1		1			7
Nelson, Thomas of Wm.	1	2	1		1	1	1	2		1			10
Newman, Francis	4	1		2		1		1	2				26
Newman, William	2	1		1	1	1	2		1				1
Newnan, Daniel			3	9									
Ogden, Jonathen			1		1		2		1	1			4
Ogden, Thomas			1			2			1				
Ogle, Benjamin		1		1									1
Ostroe, Philip	1			1				1					1
Owen, Edward			1					1					
Owen, Eleanor	1	3	2		1	2		1	1				5
Ozborn, Jerom	1			1		2			1				
Ozborn, Rhody	1			1		4			1	1			5
Padgett, Aaron		1			1		1	1		1			
Padgett, Benjamin	2	2	1	1		2		1	1				
Padgett, Cornelius	1	1		1		1		1					
Padgett, Elizabeth			2					1					2
Padgett, Henry	5	1		1		2		1					
Padgett, James		2	1		1	3	1	2		1			
Padgett, John	2	2		1		4		1	1				
Padgett, Joseph					1				1				5
Padgett, Ruth								1	2	1			
Padgett, William	1		1			1							
Peers, Aquilla				1		1		1					
Pickrell, Catherine	1					2		2					
Pickrell, Esther		1						1					
Pickrell, Gamaliel	2			1		2		1					
Pickrell, John			1			1		1					2
Pickrell, John, Sr.		2			1				1				
Pickrell, Samuel	1	1		1		3	1		1				2
Posey, Vincent	5		1	1		1		1					4
Power, Joshua	2		1	1		1	1	1					4
Pye, Edward			1	1		2		1					8

1800 CENSUS -- STATE OF MARYLAND

County: CHARLES COUNTY

District: PORT TOBACCO PARISH

Name	Males -10	10-16	16-26	26-45	+45	Females -10	10-16	16-26	26-45	+45	Free	Slaves	Total
Ratliff, Thomas	1		1					1				21	
Ray, Charles											4	1	
Redgate, Elizabeth		1							1	1		7	
Redmond, Matthias	1		1			2	1		1			15	
Reeder, Thomas H.			1	1								16	
Reeves, Hezekiah					1				1			32	
Reeves, John C.	1		1	1		1	1		1			2	
Reeves, Susanna		2				1		2		1		4	
Reeves, Thomas C.				1				1	1	1		44	
Reeves, Thomas J.	1			1		2		1				2	
Reeves, Ubgate		1			1					1		4	
Richards, Ceasar	2				1		1	1		1		6	
Richards, Samuel	1	1			1	2	1		1			1	
Richards, Thomas			1			1		1					
Richardson, Mark		1	2	1	1	2	1	1	1			4	
Richardson, William		1		1		1			1			7	
Rieder, Chloe	4	1	1			1	1	1	1				
Roberts, Henry	1			1		2		1				2	
Robertson, Elizah		1		1		1	2		1				
Robertson, Henry				1		2			1				
Robertson, James	2	2		1			1			1		8	
Robertson, William	2	1		1		1	1		1			2	
Robertson, William, Sr.	1	1			1		1	1		1		2	
Robey, Aquilla	1			1		4	1	1	1			3	
Robey, Elizabeth	2	1				1	2		1				
Robey, Hezekiah	1			1		2			1			3	
Robey, Jacob	1			1		4		1	2			1	
Robey, Jeremiah	1			1		2			1			1	
Robey, Leslie	2	1		1		1	1		1			6	
Robey, Sarah			1					1	1	1		5	
Robey, Thomas	1	2	2		1	1		1		1		3	
Robey, William, Sr. of Rd.		1	2		1			3		1			
Robey, William S.			1	1		1		1				1	
Roby, Alexander		1	2	1	1	1		1		1		6	
Roby, Ann			1					2		1		2	
Roby, Baruch		1		1		3		1					
Roby, Benjamin				1		1		2	1	1		1	
Roby, Caleb	1			1		1		1				1	
Roby, Frederick	1			1		3		1				1	
Roby, James	1			1		1	1	1				1	
Roby, Jessee	2			1		2		1					
Roby, John Acton	1	1		1		1		2	1			2	
Roby, John H.	1	1			1		1	2	1				
Roby, Keziah								1	1	1			
Roby, Leonard		1				1		1				1	
Roby, Richard						1		1		1			

1800 CENSUS -- STATE OF MARYLAND

County: CHARLES COUNTY

District: PORT TOBACCO PARISH

Name	Males -10	10-16	16-26	26-45	+45	Females -10	10-16	16-26	26-45	+45	Free	Slaves	Total
Roby, Samuel			3	1		1	1	2		1		1	
Roby, Timothy				1		1		1				2	
Roby, Townley	1			1		1		1				2	
Roby, William	1		1			1				2		3	
Rogerson, Thomas	3		2	1							1	3	
Russell, James			1	1	1					1		6	
Samuel, Roby, Jr.			1		1	1	1	1		1			
Sanders, Ann	1	1	1			1	2	1	1			8	
Sanders, Benedicta	2		1			1	2	3		1			
Sanders, Edward	1			2		2		2	1			8	
Sanders, Joseph	1		2			1		2	1	1		7	
Sanders, William		1		1		2		1		1		25	
Scott, Alexander	2		1	1				1		1	3		
Scriber, George													
Scroggen, Dorothy		1	2					1	1	1		1	
Sewall, Charles, Rev.d			2	1	2				1	1		37	
Sewall, Charles, Jr.	2				1	1	2		1			12	
Sewall, Francis			1									15	
Sherburn, Joseph			1									1	
Sherburn, William			2							1		10	
Simmes, Bennett B.	2		1			2		1			1	15	
Simmes, Charles	1	1	1			2			1			2	
Simmes, Edward					1		1		1			7	
Simmes, Eleanor			1				1	2	1	1		17	
Simmes, Francis			1					1				4	
Simmes, James	2		1			3	1		1				
Simmes, Joseph M.	1		2			2			1		1	7	
Simmes, Robert D.	1	1	1		1	3		1	1			25	
Simmons, Elizabeth						1	1	1	1				
Simms, Marmaduke					1	2		1	2	1		17	
Slater, Lettice		1										1	
Smallwood, Cassandra	2		1	1		1	2	3		1			
Smallwood, Eleanor	2		2			1				1		8	
Smallwood, Henry	1		1			2	1		1			7	
Smallwood, James			1	1								2	
Smallwood, John				1								1	
Smallwood, Leadston	3	1		1				1		1		7	
Smallwood, Mary										1		11	
Smallwood, Samuel	1	2		1		1			1			3	
Smallwood, Samuel			1			2	1						
Smallwood, Susanna		1						1		1			
Smallwood, Walter B.			1			1		1				1	
Smallwood, William M.		1		1	1					1		7	

1800 CENSUS -- STATE OF MARYLAND

County: **CHARLES COUNTY**

District: **PORT TOBACCO PARISH**

Name	\-10	10-16	16-26	26-45	+45	\-10	10-16	16-26	26-45	+45	Free	Slaves	Total
	Males					Females							
Smith, Cornelius	1	1		1		1	1	1	1				
Smith, Elexius	2			1		2			1			2	
Smith, Elizabeth								1		1		4	
Smith, James	1	1	1			1		1	1				
Smith, James	1			1		1		2		1			
Smith, Matthew	1	1			1	1			1	1		13	
Smith, Vincent	4		1					1					
Smith, Walter		1	3		1	1	1	1	1	2		14	
Smoot, William B of Thos.			2		2			1		1		13	
Spalding, Basil	1	1	1	1		3	1		2			4	
Spalding, Francis	1	1		1		3		1				3	
Spalding, George H.				1		1		1	1	1		9	
Stewart, Francis Igns.	2	1		1		2	1		1			1	
Stewart, Isaac	2			2		1	1		1	1		3	
Stewart, John B.	1			1		1	1		1			3	
Stewart, Philip	1		1	1		1		2				59	
Stewart. William	3	1	1		1		1			1		4	
Stone, Grace											5		
Stone, Michael I.	2		1	1		1		2	1			19	
Swann, Edward	1	1		1		1		1					
Swann, Samuel			1	1			1		1			2	
Swann, Walter	2	1	2	1			1	1				3	
Sweeny, Allen				1		1			1			1	
Tanch, Ann						1		1		1		4	
Thomas, Henry	1				1			1		1		3	
Thomas, Notley	1		1					1					
Thomas, William	4		1				1		1				
Thompson, Ann		2						1		1		1	
Thompson, George			2		1			1	1	1		5	
Thompson, James			1			1			1		1	5	
Thompson, John	2		1			3	1		2			6	
Thompson, John B.	1	1			1	3	1		1			21	
Thompson, Thomas		1	1		1	1		2	3	1			
Timmes, William	1	1		1		3			1			1	
Timmes, William	2			1		1		1	1				
Tubman, Richard	1		1	1		2			1			14	
Tubman, Samuel	1			1		1			1			6	
Tucker, Rhody	1	1		1		1		1	2			1	
Tueson, Robert											5	1	
Turner, Jonathan, Jr.				1				1				1	
Turner, Jonathan, Jr.		1		1	1		1	1		1		1	
Turner, Joseph	2	2	2		1	1	1	1	1		1	8	
Turner, Mary			2			1	1	1		1		20	

1800 CENSUS -- STATE OF MARYLAND

County: CHARLES COUNTY

District: PORT TOBACCO PARISH

Name	Males -10	10-16	16-26	26-45	+45	Females -10	10-16	16-26	26-45	+45	Free	Slaves	Total
Turter, George F.	3			1		1			1		2	10	
Tyar, Alexius		1	1			3	1					15	
Tyar, Francis	1	1		1		1			1	2		12	
Tyler, William	3	1			1	1	1		1	1		11	
Varden, Richard				1		2			1	1		6	
Vincent, Martha	3	1				3			2	1			
Vincent, William			2	2								1	
Ward, John of Augustine					1	2	1		1			12	
Wars, Ann		1				1			1			5	
Ware, Francis, Senr.	5			3	6	3			4	8	10	1	
Ware, Francis of Jacob	2	2		1		3			1	1			
Wars, William	1			1		2			1			1	
Wathen, Barton	1	2		1				1	1	1		3	
Wathen, Hester		1	2			1	1	1	1	2		4	
Wathen, Theophilus	1			1		1			1				
Wedding, James			1						1				
Wedding, John	1			1		1			1				
Wedding, John	1	2	1		1	3	1		1		1		
Wedding, Meshech	2		1						2				
Wedding, Philip	2	1				1	2	1		1			
Weems, John, Rev.	4	1	1	1					1			6	
Welch, Edward	3	2				1	2	1			3	4	
Wheatley, Samuel													
Wheeler, Benedict		1				1	2		1	1	1		
Wheeler, Benjamin			1			1			3			1	
Wheeler, Eleanor						1			2	1			
Wheeler, Ignatius	2					1	1		1		2	3	
Wheeler, John	1		1			1			1		1	2	
Wheeler, Joseph			1	1		1			1	1		8	
Wheeler, Luke				1				1				6	
Wheeler, William						1				1		13	
Wilkinson, Alexander, Jr.				1					1				
Wilkinson, Walter	2	1				1	2	2		1		4	
Willett, Benjamin			1	1		1		1					
Willett, George				1		1		2	1				
Willett, James	2	1	2			1	1		1			2	
Willett, William	2		1			1			1			1	
Williams, Joe (Free Blacks)											5		
Williams, John			2			1		1	2			3	
Wills, John B., Jr.			1	1								1	
Witvogle, Alexander			2									1	
Wright, John	1			1					1		1	1	

1800 CENSUS -- STATE OF MARYLAND

County: ___CHARLES COUNTY___

District: ___SAINT GEORGES PARISH___

Name	Males -10	10-16	16-26	26-45	+45	Females -10	10-16	16-26	26-45	+45	Free	Slaves	Total
Adams, Mary	2					2	1					1	
Atchison, John			1	1			1					6	
Atchison, William			1		1	2	1						
Berry, Susanna	1		1			2	1		1			3	
Boswell, Philip	2		1	1					1			1	
Brandt, Richard	1	1			1	1			1			13	
Brawner, Henry of Wm.			1					1				3	
Briscoe, Edward				1			2	2		1		17	
Briscoe, Philip T.	1			2			1	1				11	
Butler, Edw. & Gray, Henry											10		
Chapman, Susanna				3						1	11	38	
Clagett, Mary			2					1	1	1	5	19	
Clements, Bede				1							1	2	
Clements, Edward	3		1	1		1	2		1		8		
Clements, Henry of Adler			1					1				8	
Clements, John	1	1	2	2	1	1	1	2		1		9	
Clements, John of Wm.				2								4	
Clements, Zachariah	3	1	1			1			1				
Dejean, Peter					1					1		15	
Dement, William	3	2			1	1	1	1	1		1	9	
Dent, Ann									1	1		8	
Dent, George of John	3	2	1	1	1		1		1			30	
Dent, John, Genl.						1				1		24	
Dent, Theodore	2			1						1	1	6	
Dent, Thomas M.	1			1		1	2			1	1	34	
Dixon, George		1	2			1	1	1	1		1	6	
Dixon, John	1			1					1			11	
Dixon, William					1	1						6	
Downs, Charles				1				3	1			3	
Edelen, John B.	3	1		1		2	1		1			7	
Edelin, Joseph	1			1		1		1			5	4	
Fendall, Mary T.			1					1		1		10	
Fenwick, James		1	1	1	1							65	

1800 CENSUS -- STATE OF MARYLAND

County: CHARLES COUNTY

District: SAINT GEORGES PARISH

Name	\-10	10-16	16-26	26-45	+45	\-10	10-16	16-26	26-45	+45	Free	Slaves	Total
	Males					Females							
Gantt, George	2	1		1		1	1	1	1			10	
Gates, Leonard	2	1		1		1		2	1				
Gates, William	1	1	1	1		1	1		1				
Gettings, John	4	1		1					1			1	
Gettings, Thomas	2	1	1	1			1		1				
Gray, Henry & Butler, Edw.											10		
Green, Margaret									2				
Greenfield, Thomas T.			1						1	1		10	
Griffis, Thomas			1	1	1	1			1	1			
Guy, John, Sr.				1	1	1			1	1		6	
Hall, Robert C.		1		1		2			1			7	
Hamilton, Hezekiah	1			1		1		1				3	
Hamilton, Marmaduke			1	1	1			2			2	6	
Jackson, James											11		
Jameson, Walter	2		1	1		4	2		1			30	
Kemp, Samuel					1					1		3	
Kendrick, Zachariah	1		1		1				1			6	
Kerrigin, Thomas		1		2									
McAtee, Thomas, Jr.	2			1		2			1		4		
McAtee, Thomas, Sr.					1	1					2		
McPherson, Walter		1				1	1	1		1		19	
Mannery, Richard	1			1		3			1		3		
Marbury, Henry	2		1	1						1		6	
Marshall, John of Thos.				1		3			1			10	
Marshall, Thomas, Sr.				1	1	1		1		1		28	
Marshall, Thomas H.				1						1		57	
Monroe, John	1			2		1		2				2	
Monroe, Thomas				1		3		1				1	
Monroe, Thomas, Sr.					1	1						1	
Mudd, Smith	1	1				1		1	2			7	
Padgett, Elisha			1			1	1	1					
Perry, Sybell			1					2	1				
Power, John			2		1		1	2		1			
Pye, Charles	2	1	1	2		2			2		1	30	
Pye, Joseph	2			1								11	

1800 CENSUS -- STATE OF MARYLAND

County: CHARLES COUNTY

District: SAINT GEORGES PARISH

	Males					Females							
Name	-10	10-16	16-26	26-45	+45	-10	10-16	16-26	26-45	+45	Free	Slaves	Total
Rowe, John		1	1	1				2	1			11	
Rowe, William		1	2	1				1	1			6	
Rowland, John			1			1		1	1			2	
Rowland, William			2						1	1			
Savoy, William											8		
Shaw, John		1						1					
Slater, John	2		1					1					
Smallwood, Bayne			1					1				7	
Smallwood, Mary			1						1			3	
Smallwood, Thomas, Jr.	1	2				1	2	1	1		1		
Smallwood, Thomas, Sr.		1						1		1		13	
Smith, Josias		1	1			1	1	2		1			1
Smith, Simon	1	1	1			1	1	2	2	1	1	1	
Speake, Hezekiah	1		1	1		4	1		1			18	
Stewart, George	1	1		1		3	1		1			6	
Stoddert, Elizabeth									1		1	18	
Stoddert, Thomas				1					1		2	17	
Stonestreet, Henry	1	1	2	2	1	1		2			1	14	
Thompson, Henry (of Smallwood)			1			3			1		1	14	
Thompson, William	2						1	1	1				
Tubman, Henry			1					1				7	
Tubman, James	1		1					1				5	
Tubman, Samuel	1		1			1		1				6	
Ward, George M.	1		1			1	1					9	
Ward, John		1				1				1		2	
Ward, Thomas	2		1			1	1			2	1	8	
Wheeler, Edward			1									3	
Wilkinson, Alexander, Jr.			1						1			1	
Wilkinson, Alexander, Sr.					1				1		10		

1800 CENSUS -- STATE OF MARYLAND

County: **CHARLES COUNTY**

District: **TRINITY PARISH**

Name	Males -10	10-16	16-26	26-45	+45	Females -10	10-16	16-26	26-45	+45	Free	Slaves	Total
Adams, John	1	2	3		1			1		1		8	
Adams, John of George	3		1			1		1				4	
Adams, John, Free Mulatto											7		
Adams, Josias			1									21	
Adams, Walter	1		1			2	1					2	
Albritain, Charles		1		1		2	1	1		1			
Albritain, William			2		1		1	1		1			
Allen, John		1	1				1	1					
Allen, Joseph			1			1	1		1				
Amery, Samuel			2	1	1			1	1			14	
Anderson, Ann				1				1		1		1	
Anderson, Benjamin	2			1		2		1					
Anderson, Henry	2		1	2				3					
Bacchus, John - A free Black			1				1		1	1	1		
Barker, Joseph, Jr.		1	1					2		2		6	
Barker, Joseph, Sen.	3			1		2			1			12	
Barron, Margaret									1				
Beane, Leonard	2			1		2	2		1			4	
Beavin, Basil W.	2		1	1		2	1	1	1			2	
Beavin, Benjamin		1	1		1			2		1		10	
Beavin, John	2	3	1		1	1	1	2				4	
Beavin, Richard, Sr.			1	1		1		1		1		4	
Beavin, Richard (of Basil)			2		1			1				4	
Beavin, Walter	3			1		2		1				7	
Beddo, James											9		
Billingsley, Thomas	1		1	2		1	1	1				3	
Black, Elizabeth	3		1			1	1	1					
Blackstock, Robert	2	2	1	1		1		1				1	
Bleafin, Samuel			1		1			2		1			
Boarman, Charles	3		1			1			1			12	
Boarman, James			1			3		1				8	
Boarman, John, Jr.	2		1			3	1	1				8	
Boarman, John H.	2	1	1		1	2		1				9	
Boarman, Joseph of Leon'd.	2		1			3	1	1				17	
Boarman, Joseph of Ralph	1		1			2		1				6	
Boarman, Mary								2	1			4	
Boarman, Michael			2						1			6	
Boarman, Milburn	1		1			1	1					1	
Boarman, Raphael				1		2			1			20	
Boarman, Raphael of Thos. James		1		1		1			3			17	
Boarman, Teresa								1	1			28	
Boarman, Thomas, Jr.		1		3			1					2	
Boarman, Thomas I.	1		3	1	1		1					5	

1800 CENSUS -- STATE OF MARYLAND

County: CHARLES COUNTY

District: TRINITY PARISH

Name	Males -10	10-16	16-26	26-45	+45	Females -10	10-16	16-26	26-45	+45	Free	Slaves	Total
Bond, Thomas			2	1				2				5	
Bond, Walter	2		1					1				2	
Boone, James	1	3		1		1		3	1			3	
Boteler, Henderson S.			1					1				5	
Bowen, John	1		1					1					
Bowen, Thomas			1			1	1	1					
Bowling, Catherine								1	1	1		10	
Bowling, John			1			3	2	1				3	
Bowling, Marsham	1		1	1				1				23	
Bowling, Thomas				1								9	
Bowling, William				1		2		1				1	
Bradford, Eleanor								1		1	1	3	
Brady, Owen	1			1		3	2		2	1		1	
Brameil, Jonathan	1		1	1		1		1				2	
Brameil, Reuben			1			2		1					
Brameil, William		1		1			1	1	1			1	
Brandt, Charles			1	1			2		1			14	
Brayfield, Robert	3	1		1				1	1				
Brents, Miss			1					1	6		1	15	
Brightwell, Richard	2		1			3			1		3	7	
Briscoe, William D.	2		2			1		3	2			27	
Brookbank, William	4		1			1			1		1	8	
Brown, Henrietta											8		
Bryan, Amney			1						2			1	
Burch, Ann	1	2				2	1	2	1			6	
Burch, Edward				1		3		1		1		13	
Burch, Edward of Ed.			1			1		1	1	1		8	
Burch, Jessee of Edw.			2	2	1					1		4	
Burch, Jonathan			1	1								11	
Burch, Justinian	5		1	2		3		1		1		16	
Burrage, Edward	2		1					1				1	
Burrage, Ninian				1					1	1		5	
Burrows, Elisha	1			1		2		1	1				
Burtles, William	2			1		2		1				8	
Butler, John											6		
Butler, Milley											5		
Butler, Philis											6		
Cahooe, Ignatius						1	2	1	2	1			
Cahooe, Thomas		1				1		2		1			
Canter, Elizabeth			1							1			
Canter, Elizah		1		1		1			1			5	
Canter, James		1	1			1	2			1		3	
Canter, Leonard	3	1	1			2		1				6	

1800 CENSUS -- STATE OF MARYLAND

County: CHARLES COUNTY

District: TRINITY PARISH

Name	Males -10	10-16	16-26	26-45	+45	Females -10	10-16	16-26	26-45	+45	Free	Slaves	Total
Carricoe, Henry	4		1			1		1		1			
Carricoe, Joseph	2			1		3	1	1	1				
Carricoe, Mary Ann		1	1					1	2			5	
Carricoe, Monica									1	1			
Carricoe, William	1		1	1			2	1				4	
Carter, Jessee			1	1								5	
Cartwright, Peter	1		1			3		1				4	
Cartwright, Samuel	5	3		1					2		1	5	
Cartwright, Susanna			1						2			6	
Ching, Thomas		1	1	1	1	1			1			2	
Chunn, Amos		1		1		2			1			4	
Chunn, Deborah		1							1		1	6	
Chunn, Lancelot						1	1		1	1		4	
Clarke, Henry	2	2				1	3	2	1	1		1	
Clements, Benedict		4				1	2			1		2	
Collins, George											4		
Compton, William						1				1		4	
Compton, Wilson	2			1		2			2			15	
Cooke, Alexander			1			1		1				10	
Cooksey, Henry		3	1	1		1	1	1	1			14	
Cooksey, Isaac	1			1		3			1			1	
Cooksey, Jonathan		1		1	1		1			2		4	
Cooksey, Justinian	1		1			1		1	3	1			
Cooksey, Ledstone S.	3	2	1	1			1	1	1				
Cope, James											2		
Corry, William	4			1		1			1			15	
Curtis, Joseph											4		
David, John B. M. Rev^d.				2							1	19	
Davis, Benjamin		1		1		3		1					
Davis, George		2		1			1	1	1				
Davis, Jeremiah				1					1				
Davis, Jessee	4				1	2			1			3	
Davis, Joshua	1			1		1		1	1		1	1	
Davis, Joshua	1			1		1	1		1			1	
Davis, Kenelm	1	1		1		3	1		1	1			
Davis, Leonard	2		1			2		1				2	
Davis, Mary	2	1	1			1	1	3				1	
Davis, Philip			1			1		1	1			10	
Davis, Sarah		1					1	3	1			4	
Davis, William		1				1	2	1				1	
Davis, Zaccheus				1		1		1	1	1	1	10	
Demarr, Joshua	2	2	1			1	2	1	1	1	1	2	
Demarr, Melcolm	1			1			1					1	
Demarr, William	3	1		1		2		1					
Dement, Edward	2	2	1	1		1	1		1				

1800 CENSUS -- STATE OF MARYLAND

County: CHARLES COUNTY

District: TRINITY PARISH

Name	M -10	M 10-16	M 16-26	M 26-45	M +45	F -10	F 10-16	F 16-26	F 26-45	F +45	Free	Slaves	Total
Dent, Benjamin					1	2		1			1	2	
Dent, Gideon	1	1		1	1	3	1		1				10
Dent, Hatch	3	1	1	1		1	2		1				13
Dent, John Brewer	1	1		1		2			1				7
Dent, Jonathan				2		1		1					2
Dent, Judith	2					3	1		1				13
Dent, Mary M.	2	1							2	1			3
Dent, Peter			1	1		1				1			4
Dent, Titus	2					1	1	3	1	1			3
Dent, Victory		1							1	1	1		4
Dent, William	1			2		1		1	1		1		5
Dent, Zachariah	2	1		1		3			1				7
Dixon, John G.	3			1				2		1			2
Dixon, Samuel						1				1			3
Dixon, Susannah								1	1		1		
Douglass, Benjamin	4		1			1		1	2				10
Duggins, Robert	3			1		3			1				1
Dyer, George						1		1		1			9
Dyson, George				1					1				6
Dyson, Gerard	1	2	1	1		1	2	1	1	1			3
Dyson, Walter	1			1				1	1		1		22
Edelin, Edward	1	1		1		1			1		1		12
Edelin, Francis	1	2		1	1	2	1	1	1				18
Edelin, John of Edw'd.	4			1		1	1		1				19
Edelin, Leonard				1									
Edelin, Ozwald	3			1		1	1	1			3	4	
Edelin, Philip				1							4	3	
Edelin, Richard, Sr.			1		1				1				31
Edelin, Susanna	1		2	1		1	1		1	1			4
Edelin, Susanna				1					1				5
Edwards, Hezekiah			1	1	1			2	2	1			5
Edwards, Sarah	1						2	4		2			5
Estep, John, Junr.			1	2				1					6
Estep, John, Senr.	1	1	1		1	3			2				10
Estep, Philemon	2			1		2			1				10
Evans, William	2			1		2		1					
Farrand, Elizabeth		1							3	1			1
Farrand, Timothy		2				1	1		1	1			
Farrand, William				1									2
Farrand, Zephaniah	3	1		2		3			1				2
Forbes, John	2	2	2	2		2	1	1					17

1800 CENSUS -- STATE OF MARYLAND

County: CHARLES COUNTY

District: TRINITY PARISH

Name	Males -10	10-16	16-26	26-45	+45	Females -10	10-16	16-26	26-45	+45	Free	Slaves	Total
Gardiner, Aloysia	1	1	1			1	1		1			12	
Gardiner, Charles	1			1		2	1		1	1		15	
Gardiner, Henry		1	1	1	1	2			1			26	
Gardiner, Ignatius	3	2			1	4			1			23	
Gardiner, John				1	1	1						10	
Gardiner, John F.					1	2						18	
Gardiner, Joseph	3		1	1		1		1				16	
Gardiner, William		1	1		1	1	2			1		10	
Gary, Francis	1		1		1	1	2	1		1			
Gibbons, George					1							7	
Gibbons, Martha	1	1	1			2	1		1			16	
Gibbons, Nehemiah	4	1		1	1		2	1	1			4	
Gibbons, Stephen				1								8	
Gibson, John	1		2		1	1	2	1		1	1		
Gibson, William			1					1					
Gill, Elizabeth		1	2			1	1	1		1		7	
Gill, John			1		1	3	2		1				
Glasgow, William	1			1		1	1		1				
Goldsmith, Townley	2			1				1		1			
Good, Roswell	1	2			1	2	2	2	1				
Good, William	1		1			1			1			2	
Gray, George	1	2			1			2		1			
Gray, James					1	1	1		1	1	1		
Greenwell, William			1	1		4			1			5	
Guy, Matthew			1			1		2					
Guy, Moses	4	1			1			2	1				
Hagan, Joseph of Wm.	2		1			1			1			10	
Hancock, Abraham						1	1	1	1			4	
Hancock, William	3	2	1			1		1	4	1		8	
Harbin, Nailor	3			1		1	1		1		1		
Harbin, Rezin	1		1					1				2	
Harbin, Rosella	2			1		1			1				
Harbin, Zephaniah W.	3	1	1	1		1			1				
Hardesty, Richard G.			1	2				1				3	
Harrison, John				1		2			1			2	
Harrison, William	2	1	1		1		1	1	1			15	
Haw, John S.	3			1					1			17	
Hazard, Ann	1					1			1				
Hazard, Michael		1	1				1	3					
Hickey, Francis		1	1		1	3	1		1			8	
Higdon, Eleazer D.				2		1						7	
Higdon, Patty	1					1	1		1	1		2	
Higges, Bernard		1		1				2					
Higges, Hanson		1		1				2					

1800 CENSUS -- STATE OF MARYLAND

County: CHARLES COUNTY

District: TRINITY PARISH

| | Males | | | | | Females | | | | | | | |
Name	-10	10-16	16-26	26-45	+45	-10	10-16	16-26	26-45	+45	Free	Slaves	Total
Hill, Sarah											5		
Hunt, Elijah	1	1		1		1				1			
Hunt, Gladden	2	1		1		2	2	1	1		1	5	
Hunt, Susanna			1			1		1	1				
Hunt, Townshend W.				1									3
Huntington, John	1	1		1		3	1						
Hutchison, John			1					1		1			13
Jackson, Abednego												2	
Jackson, John												4	
Jackson, Samuel												6	
James (a free black)												2	
Jameson, Henry I.					1							2	4
Jameson, Jesse	1		1			1			1				4
Jameson, Raphael			1			5		1					15
Jameson, Samuel	1			1		2		1					18
Jameson, Thomas				1		1		1					13
Jenkins, Isaac	1	1						1	1				
Jenkins, Isaac	1	1						1	1				
John, (a free black)												2	
Johnson, Alexander				1		1		1					2
Johnson, Hewett	1	2	1		1	3	1		1				5
Johnson, James			1		1			1	1	1			
Johnson, John, Jr.				1	1			1					4
Johnson, John, Jr.				1					1				4
Johnson, Joseph				1		3			1				
Johnson, Joseph		1	1		1	2		3	1				4
Johnson, Joseph of Hewit	3	1	1		1	1		1	1				7
Johnson, Mary	1							1	1				13
Johnson, Mary										1		2	4
Jones, George	1	1				1							
Jones, James		1		1									
Kennick, John	2			1		2			2		1	1	
Kidwell, William			1			1	1						
King, Judith							1	2	1	1			3
King, Vincent			1		1	2		1	1				1
King, Williamson					1			2		1			9
Kusick, Elizabeth	1					1			1	1			4
Lancaster, Thomas	3	2	1					1		2			14
Langley, John			1			3			1				6
Leech, Asahel		1											6
Leech, Thomas	1		1		1	1		1					6

1800 CENSUS -- STATE OF MARYLAND

County: CHARLES COUNTY

District: TRINITY PARISH

Name	Males -10	10-16	16-26	26-45	+45	Females -10	10-16	16-26	26-45	+45	Free	Slaves	Total
Levy, Anthony	4	1		1			1		2			3	
Little, Peter, Jr.				1		2	2		1				
Lomax, Thomas			2		1					1			
Lyon, Elizabeth	1	3				2			1			3	
Lyon, Henry, Jr.	1	1	1		1		1	2	1	1		10	
Lyon, James	1			1			1	1				2	
Lyon, Jane	1		2	1			2	3	1	1		2	
Lyon, Leonard			2	1	1	1			1			18	
McPherson, Alexander			3		1	3	3	1		1		30	
McPherson, Charles	3		2	1		2		1		2		18	
Maddox, Allison				1				1				2	
Maddox, John			1					1				2	
Marshall, Benjamin			1	1	1			2	2	1	1	6	
Mason, Richard		1		1	1		1			1		31	
Matthews, Ann	4					2		1				8	
Mattingly, George	2		3	1		1		1				2	
Mattingly, Zachariah	1	1			1		2	2		1			
Medley, Enoch				1	1							5	
Meede, Edward				1									
Meede, Sarah							1	1	1			1	
Merryman, James	3			1					2			2	
Millar, Alexander	3	1		1				1				1	
Mitchell, Susanne		2							1			13	
Mollohon, William I.	1		1	1				1					
Monroe, John					1	2	3		1			2	
Montgomery, Eleanor			1	1		1				2			
Moore, George	1		1	1			1		1			4	
Moran, Andrew				1					1			6	
Moran, Caleb				1								5	
Moran, Charles	1			1		2			1			5	
Moran, Elijah	1			1		1			1			2	
Moran, John, Senr.			1	1	1	1	1					19	
Moran, John of Gabr.				1		1			1		1	1	
Moran, John of Mevl.	1			1					1			4	
Moran, John of Peter	3	1	2		1		1	3		1		4	
Moran, Jonathan		1	1		1				1			4	
Moran, Leonard	1		1		1		1					1	
Moran, Luke	2	1	1		3	1		1				1	
Moran, Meveral, Jr.			1		1				1			5	
Moran, Meveral, Sr.				1					1			6	
Moran, William of Gabu.			2									3	
Morriss, Ann	1				2				1				
Morriss, Joshua		2	1		1	1		1					
Morton, Elizabeth	1	1			1	1		2				13	

1800 CENSUS -- STATE OF MARYLAND

County: CHARLES COUNTY

District: TRINITY PARISH

Name	Males -10	10-16	16-26	26-45	+45	Females -10	10-16	16-26	26-45	+45	Free	Slaves	Total
Morton, George	2	2	1		1	1	1		1			18	
Morton, Joseph	2	2	1		1	2		1	1			12	
Morton, Mary			1							1		2	
Mudd, Bennett			1	1	1			1	2			19	
Mudd, Henry of Thos.					2	1	1	2				14	
Mudd, Henry T.	4	1				1	1	2	1			7	
Mudd, Jane	2						1					11	
Mudd, Mary							1	2	1	1		7	
Mudd, Walter			1			1		1	1	1		5	
Murphy, Walter	1	1		1		2			1				
Murray, Edward I.	2	1		2				2		1			
Nailor, James			1				1		1			4	
Nalley, Barnabas		1				1			1				
Nalley, Gustavus	4					1	2		1			9	
Nally, Thomas, Sr.			1	1	1					1		4	
Newberry, John				1		1			1			2	
Newgent, Jeremiah	1			1		3	2		1				
Newman, William											6		
O'Bryan, Bazel	1	2				1	2	1					
O'Bryan, Mary Ann			1					1		1		1	
Oliver, James			1	1						1	1	1	
Oliver, William	3		2			1	1	1	1	1			
Overton, Caleb											11		
Ozborn, Ann			2			2			2				
Ozborn, Thomas						1				1		3	
Paddy, John	2	2		1					1				
Parker, Henry	1		2				1						
Parker, Jonathan	2	1	1		1	1		1		1		2	
Parnham, John			2	1		1	1	2		1		52	
Perry, Edward	1					1		1	1			2	
Perry, Hugh		1	1		1			1	1	1		7	
Pierce, John		2		1					2			2	
Pile, Henry, Rev'd.			1	1	1						1	44	
Posey, Elizabeth			1							2		5	
Posey, Harrison	2		1	1					1			3	
Poston, Bartholomew				1		1	1		1			7	
Power, Jessee		1		1		2			1			3	
Proctor, Basil											2	1	
Proctor, Bazel											2	1	
Proctor, Elizabeth				1							3		

1800 CENSUS -- STATE OF MARYLAND

County: CHARLES COUNTY

District: TRINITY PARISH

Name	\-10	10-16	16-26	26-45	+45	\-10	10-16	16-26	26-45	+45	Free	Slaves	Total
	Males					Females							
Proctor, Isaac											6		
Proctor, James											7		
Proctor, Thomas											3		
Proctor, William											5	1	
Queen, Mary											5	17	
Rawlings, Elizabeth	2						1	2	1	1			
Ray, James											7		
Reeves, Lyddia			2						1			7	
Rencher, John	1						1	3	1			6	
Richards, Amney Jane								3	1			4	
Richards, Paulsias				1		1			1			2	
Robertson, Benjamin	1		1	1		2		1				1	
Robertson, Thomas				1						1		2	
Robey, Joshua	1		1			2		1	2			3	
Rutter, Joseph				1						1			
Sansberrie, Nicholas			2									15	
Scallion, Peter	1					1		2	1				
Scott, Joshua											2		
Scott, Samuel			1	1				1	1			10	
Scott, William				3		1			1		1	3	
Simmes, Mark		2	1			1	1	2		2		10	
Simpson, Catherine	2						2	2					
Simpson, John Lowe				1		1	1	1					
Simpson, Joseph				1			2	1				11	
Simpson, Margarett							2	1					
Simpson, Thomas M.	2			1			2		1	1		6	
Sinclair, Mary							1			1		1	
Slye, Henrietta	1			1			1	2		1		11	
Smith, Charles S.	3			2			1		1			18	
Smith, Henry		1	1	1			1			2		24	
Smith, John of John						1					1	9	
Smith, Vernon	2	2				1	3	1	1	1			
Smith, Walter				1		1						4	
Smoot, Ann			2						1		1	20	
Smoot, Charles, Dr.			2				1		2			6	
Smoot, Hendley		1				1		1	2	1		14	
Smoot, John N.	1					1		2	2	1		11	
Smoot, Mary									2	1		3	
Smoot, Rezine	1	1	1					2				7	
Smoot, William B. of Chs.	2	1				1	1	2	1			27	

1800 CENSUS -- STATE OF MARYLAND

County: CHARLES COUNTY

District: TRINITY PARISH

Name	Males -10	10-16	16-26	26-45	+45	Females -10	10-16	16-26	26-45	+45	Free	Slaves	Total
Sothoron, Benjamin	1				1			1				7	
Sothoron, Henry			1	1				1	1			9	
Sothoron, Thomas L.				2				2				7	
Sothoron, Zachariah of Henry			2	1				1				10	
Sothoron, Zachariah of Levin				1		1		1				6	
Stewart, Henry	4	1		1		2			1				
Stone, Matthew				1									
Suit, John			1	1				1	1			1	
Suit, Thomas of Dent	3	1		1		1	1		1			1	
Suit, Walter			1		1			1		1		3	
Summers, George	2	1			1	1	1		1			5	
Swann, Chloe		1					1		1				
Swann, Mary	2		1			3			1			5	
Swann, Richard											5		
Swann, Thomas	1			1		2	4	3	1				
Swann, Thomas, Jr.				1		1		1				7	
Swann, Zachariah, Jr.				1					2				
Swann, Zachariah, Sr.		2	2		1			1					
Taylor, John	1					1		1	1			2	
Taylor, Rebecca						2	1		1	1			
Taylor, William	3	1		1				1				1	
Tench, Leonard	1		1			2			1		1	1	
Thomas, Caleb				1		1	2		1			11	
Thomas, Catharine			1	2				2	1	1		5	
Thomas, Henry											1	2	
Thomas, James			1			2	1		1			14	
Thomas, Nathan		1				1		1	1			5	
Thomas, William W.			1	1				1	1			6	
Thompson, Henry											10		
Thompson, Robert			1	1		1		1				2	
Thorne, Absalom		1	1		1					1		7	
Tippett, Eli	1		1			6		1					
Turner, Randolph	2		1	1		2	2	5	1			1	
Turner, Samuel, Jr.	1			1		2			1			1	
Turner, Samuel, Sr.				1	1	1		2	1			3	
Turner, William	1	1	2	1	1	2		1	1			11	
Turner, William, Jr.	1		1					1				1	
Turner, William of Edw'd.		1						1				5	
Venables, Mary				1				1	2	1		7	
Wallace, Cornelius	1					1	1	1				3	
Wallace, James		1										7	

1800 CENSUS -- STATE OF MARYLAND

County: **CHARLES COUNTY**

District: **TRINITY PARISH**

Name	Males -10	10-16	16-26	26-45	+45	Females -10	10-16	16-26	26-45	+45	Free	Slaves	Total
Wallace, Richard					1			1	1			6	
Ware, E. Nicholas	2			1		1		1	1				
Waters, Edward	3	1		1		1		1					
Waters, Frances	2	1	1	1				2	2			1	
Waters, Gustavus	3	2		2		2	1		1			4	
Waters, James		1	1		1			1	1	1		4	
Waters, James, Jr.	4	1		1		1			1	1		4	
Waters, John, Jr.			1		1	1		1				2	
Waters, John C.			1	1	1						2	7	
Waters, Joseph	1	1	1			1		1					
Waters, Randolph	1			1		3	1	1				2	
Waters, Thomas, Senr.		1	1		1	1	1	1	1			19	
Waters, Zephaniah	1	1		1		2	2	1		1		2	
Wathen, Baker		1		1		3			1			2	
Wathen, Barton	2	3		1		5			1			1	
Wathen, Bennett		1	1		1			2		1	1	4	
Wathen, Bennett, Jr.	1			1					1		2		
Wathen, Clement				1	1			2	4	1		2	
Wathen, Eleanor	1		1	1		1		1	1				
Wathen, Hudson	2			2				2				1	
Wathen, John B.			1	1		3	1		2		1	4	
Wathen, John S.	1			1				1	1			1	
Wathen, Mary		1							3	1			
Wathen, Thomas		1							1			2	
Watson, Cornelius	3	1		1					1				
Watson, James G.	3	1		2		1	1		1			18	
Wells, Martin	2	1			1	1	1		1			10	
Wheatley, Francis				1	1					1		10	
Wilder, Margaret			1							1		6	
Wilkinson, Ann		1				3	1	1	1		1	24	
Wilkinson, William			1					1				3	
Williams, Francis				1		1		1				1	
Winter, Elizabeth	2							1	1		1	21	
Winter, Jane	1	1				3		4		2		33	
Wood, Benjamin	2		1					1	2			1	
Wood, Benjamin, Jr.				1				1				5	
Wood, Benjamin, Sr.			1		1				3		4	5	
Wood, Henry	2		1						1			4	
Wood, Leonard, Sr.			1			1			1	2		16	
Wood, Leonard of Beh.						1	1	1			1		
Wood, Peter, Junr.			1			1						16	
Wright, John W.	2			1				1				3	
Wright, Joseph, Junr.	5	1		1				1				3	

1800 CENSUS -- STATE OF MARYLAND

County: CHARLES COUNTY

District: WILLIAM & MARY PARISH

Name	Males -10	10-16	16-26	26-45	+45	Females -10	10-16	16-26	26-45	+45	Free	Slaves	Total
......, Philip		1		1	1					1	1		
Adams, Jenny											5		
Baker, Milley	1					2	1						
Bateman, George			1				1						
Bateman, Jerrell	3			1			1	1				2	
Bateman, Mary	1	1	1			1	1	1					
Bateman, Richard	1	1		2		1	2						
Boarman, Edward						1		1				4	
Bowen, Mark						1	2	3	1			11	
Bradley, John			1			1	2	1	1			3	
Brandt, James			1									9	
Brokinbrough, John, Revd.			1					1			1	3	
Brooke, Ann							1	1					
Brooke, Richard			1			1		1	1				
Brown, James	2		1	1				1				5	
Bruce, John		1				1	3		1			19	
Bruce, William	1	1				1	2	1				7	
Burgess, Thomas						1		1	1	1		3	
Butler, Betsey											5		
Butler, Charles											7		
Butler, Henry											7		
Butler, Lewis											5		
Butler, Sarah											7		
Campbell, John, Esqr.			1	1		1		2				35	
Chunn, Charles			1				2	3	1			3	
Collins, Samuel											9		
Collins, Samuel, Jr.											10		
Collins, Samuel, Sr.											2		
Connell, Dennis		1		1		2	1		1				
Contee, Benjamin	2			1		1	1		1	2		34	
Cope, Thomas	1	1		1	1			1	1				
Cottrell, Ann			1							1		18	
Cottrell, Burford			1		1	1	1					17	
Crain, Robert	1			2		4			1	1		47	
Crismond, Martha	1					1			1				
Darrett, Wilson				1		1		1	1			3	
Dent, Eleanor						1			2			20	
Dent, George				1								8	
Dent, Henry					1	1		1				13	
Digges, Edward	1			1		1			1	1		16	
Digges, Henry				1		2		1				16	

1800 CENSUS -- STATE OF MARYLAND

County: **CHARLES COUNTY**

District: **WILLIAM & MARY PARISH**

Name		Males					Females					Free	Slaves	Total
	-10	10-16	16-26	26-45	+45	-10	10-16	16-26	26-45	+45			
Duley, Elizabeth	1	2				1		2	1			2	
Dutton, Notley, Jr.	1	2			2	3			1			2	
Dutton, Notley, Sr.					1				1			22	
Dutton, Thomas			1	1								1	
Farr, Mary						1	3		1			2	
Fearson, Joseph	4	1	1		1		1	2	2	1			
Fendall, Benjamin, Dr.	1	3		1			1		2			24	
Fenwick, Nicholas			1					1				8	
Ferrell, Leonard		1		1				2				4	
Ford, Elizabeth	1	1		1		2	1	3		1		12	
Fowler, Ann		1	1					1	1	1		21	
Glover, John P.	2		1	1		2		1				11	
Goldy, Elias	2			1		2	1	1				11	
Goodrick, Elijah		2	1			1		1				4	
Goodrick, Walter	4		1	1			2	1				4	
Grigges, William		1		1					2			2	
Guy, Sarah						2	1			1		2	
Hall, John											6		
Hamersley, Henry						1		1				19	
Hancock, Josias		1				1					1	4	
Handy, John											4		
Harris, Thomas, Col.		2		1				2	1	1		30	
Hayden, Barton	1			1		1		1				3	
Higdon, Francis	3		2	1	1	1		1	1			3	
Hobert, Edward			1	1			1	1		1		4	
Holmes, William			1	1					2	1		19	
Hungerford, Violetta			1				1			1		34	
Jenkins, Ann	1								1			1	
Jenkins, Charles		1										4	
Jenkins, Charles		1										4	
Jenkins, Ignatius	1	1		1					1			1	
Jenkins, Ignatius	1							1					
Jenkins, Thomas, Capt.	2	2	2		1	1	1		1			30	
Jenkins, William	1	1		1		1	1		1				
Johnson, Rachael	1					1		1		1			
Jonas, Barr, a free black											3	2	

County: ___CHARLES COUNTY___

District: ___WILLIAM & MARY PARISH___

Name	Males					Females					Free	Slaves	Total
	-10	10-16	16-26	26-45	+45	-10	10-16	16-26	26-45	+45			
Kersey, Daniel	4	1		1					1				
Kimbo, Nathaniel				1		2	1	1				2	
King, Aquilla	1	1	1	1		2	1		1		2	3	
Kirpatrick, William					1							2	
Laidler, John				1		3	2		1			13	
Laidler, Robert			1		1	1			1			25	
Lancaster, Charles						1						10	
Lancaster, Francis	1					1			1			15	
Lancaster, John, Capt.	2	2				1	2	1	1	1		24	
Lancaster, Mary						1		1		1		28	
Latimer, Ann		2	1						2		1	12	
Latimer, Samuel	2					1	2		1			17	
Latimer, William	2					1		1	1			8	
Lawrence, William	3	1		1			1	1	1			2	
Leigh, Christopher	1	1				1		2			1		
Leigh, Lewis	3					1			1			9	
Luckett, Thomas	1		2	1		2			1			7	
Maddox, Eleanor			1	1					1		2	10	
Maddox, John	3			1	1	2	1		2			22	
Mahorney, Clement	2	1	1			1			1	1			
Marshall, Ann			1				1		2			9	
Marshall, John, Major		1				1			1			24	
Martin, Huse	3					1	1	2	1			25	
Matthews, George											4		
Mattingly, Raphael	1			1		2			1			2	
Minitree, Charles			1									1	
Minitree, Paul	1	1		1		2	1	1	1			6	
Morris, Joshua	1	2		1		1	1	1	1				
Murray, Philip A.			1		1		2	2	1	1			
Neale, Ann		2					1	4	1	1		15	
Neale, Bennett	1					3			1			14	
Neale, James			3	1			1	1				19	
Neale, Jeremiah	1			1		2	1	1				3	
Neale, John	1			1	1		1	1	1			12	
Nettle, James, Jr.	1			1			3		1			4	
Nettle, James, Sr.				1			3	1		1		6	
Nettle, Matthew			1			3		1				2	
Newton, William			2			1		2				1	

1800 CENSUS -- STATE OF MARYLAND

County: CHARLES COUNTY

District: WILLIAM & MARY PARISH

Name	Males					Females					Free	Slaves	Total
	-10	10-16	16-26	26-45	+45	-10	10-16	16-26	26-45	+45			
Oakley, John	1	2	2		1		2		1			2	
Oakley, Joseph	2			1		1	3		1	1		5	
Penn, Jezreil	2	1	1	1	2		1	2	1			14	
Penn, John	2	1		1		2		2	1				
Penn, Mark	2	1		1	2	2		1					
Philpot, Elizabeth				1				1	1	1		13	
Posey, Margaret	2	1	3					2	1			20	
Posey, Samuel	1			1				1	1	1		16	
Posey, Thomas				1				1	1			6	
Proctor, Elexius											7		
Quade, James				1			2		1			15	
Ratliff, Ann	2	2	1					3	1				
Robinson, William	2		2		1	1	4	1	1				
Roby, Charles	1			1			3		1			14	
Shaw, Edward			1					1				3	
Shaw, William F.	1			1				1				18	
Shorter, Charity											3		
Simmes, Mary			2					2	1			10	
Simms, James			1				1	1				3	
Simpson, James	1	1	1	1				1	1		1	1	
Smith, James		2	1	1		1		1					
Smith, John		3		1		2	1		1				
Smith, Samuel			1	1					1			1	
Smoot, Alexander S.	3		1	1					1	1		25	
Smoot, Horatio	1		1			1			1			14	
Smoot, William G.	2			1			2		1			7	
Still, Ignatius											4		
Stone, John K.	2			1		1		1	1			6	
Stubblefield, Simon				2									
Swann, Polly											3		
Thomas, Eleanor											2		
Thomas, George				1				1		1		10	
Thompkins, Martha										1	1		
Thompkins, William	3					1	1	1	1			9	
Thompson, James	1			2		1			1			17	
Tompkins, John, Sr.	1	1				1	2	1	1	1	1	4	
Turvey, Joshua						1	3	1				2	

1800 CENSUS -- STATE OF MARYLAND

County: __CHARLES COUNTY__

District: __WILLIAM & MARY PARISH__

Name	Males -10	10-16	16-26	26-45	+45	Females -10	10-16	16-26	26-45	+45	Free	Slaves	Total
Vincent, William	3			1		1	1	2				13	
Wilder, James				1				1	1			11	
Wilder, John B.		1			1			1	1			4	
Wiseman, John											5		
Wiseman, Zachariah		1		1			2	1	1				
Wood, Gerard, Dr.	1			1		2		1	1			11	
Yates, Henry S.			1	1	1							42	
Yates, Robert	2	1					2	1				10	
Yates, Townley, Dr.	1	1				1	1	2	2			36	

The listings for the 1800 Census were transcribed, compiled and prepared by Mrs. Gladys Keen, J. Harrison Daniels, and George Ely Russell, all members of the Maryland Genealogical Society. It was originally printed in 1967 as a separate copyrighted publication of the Maryland Genealogical Society.